Anxiously Attached

"Jessica Baum's forthrightness, vulnerability, and clinical sensitivity provide the foundation for a powerful journey of growth for anyone who has experienced a nonsecure form of attachment formally known as 'ambivalent' and publicly referred to as being 'anxiously attached.' The science of relational connections between child and parent, known as attachment research, reveals a preoccupation and revving up of our drive for connection that has the inner experience of learned anxiety and uncertainty. Because of neural plasticity, we can focus our attention to build neural networks that in our childhood did not have the chance to grow how they might have to give us equanimity even in the face of relational challenges. Now you can learn to cultivate the skills of inner soothing provided in this excellent guide—and you'll discover how to 'learn' or 'earn' security in this science-backed yet practical set of steps to build the capacities that were not developed in your youth. Welcome to the challenge—and opportunity—to transform your life from the inside out!"
—Daniel J. Siegel, MD, executive director, Mindsight Institute;
clinical professor, UCLA School of Medicine;
New York Times bestselling author of *IntraConnected*,
Aware, and *Mind*, and coauthor of
Parenting from the Inside Out

"Jessica wholeheartedly puts her full self into everything she does, and this book is a gift to your true self. Self-love is the foundation for a fulfilling and balanced life. Readers, you're in for a beautiful treat."
—Shannon Kaiser, author of *The Self-Love Experiment*

"In a world of empty promises and shallow veneers, Jessica Baum has written a book that delivers what it promises. In *Anxiously Attached*, she takes her readers on a healing journey that enables them to understand why they are plagued by relational insecurities and gives them concrete tools to repair the issues of their past and embrace a future filled with meaningful and rich relationships with themselves and others." —Dr. Paul L. Hokemeyer, author of *Fragile Power*

"Jessica Baum is a modern and energetic author who brings fresh insights and language to learning how to love oneself and others. Her book contains powerful information and original ways of thinking about self-care. I highly recommend it."

—John Lee, author of *The Half-Lived Life*
and *Growing Yourself Back Up*

"Jessica's work is a breath of fresh air. Blending both a clinical and spiritual approach, this book helps us understand the nuances of modern relationships and provides a no-nonsense roadmap for healing our relationships by healing ourselves."

—James McCrae, author of *Sh#t Your Ego Says*

"Jessica walks you through a spiritual journey in this book. *Anxiously Attached* covers complex topics around codependency, and the way she explains them makes these topics easy to understand. Jessica's work helps you feel supported through all levels of transformation."

—Amy Leigh Mercree, bestselling author of *A Little Bit of Goddess*
and *A Little Bit of Mindfulness*

"Learning to attach to others in a healthy way is one of the greatest gifts you can give yourself. *Anxiously Attached* gives you the tools you need to take that step. Jessica empowers you to grab hold of your inner security, which will transform your most important relationships."

—R. Scott Gornto, PhD, MDiv, LMFT, CST,
author of *The Stories We Tell Ourselves*

Anxiously Attached

BECOMING MORE SECURE
IN LIFE AND LOVE

JESSICA BAUM, LMHC

a TarcherPerigee book

tarcher**perigee**

An imprint of Penguin Random House LLC
penguinrandomhouse.com

Illustrations by Monika Jasnauskaite

TarcherPerigee with tp colophon is a registered trademark of Penguin Random House LLC.

Most TarcherPerigee books are available at special quantity discounts for bulk
purchase for sales promotions, premiums, fund-raising, and educational needs.
Special books or book excerpts also can be created to fit specific needs.
For details, write: SpecialMarkets@penguinrandomhouse.com.

Library of Congress Cataloging-in-Publication Data

Names: Baum, Jessica, author.
Title: Anxiously attached: becoming more secure in life and love / Jessica Baum, LMHC.
Description: [New York]: TarcherPerigee, [2022]
Identifiers: LCCN 2022004971 (print) | LCCN 2022004972 (ebook) |
ISBN 9780593331064 (hardcover) | ISBN 9780593331071 (epub)
Subjects: LCSH: Attachment behavior. | Anxiety. |
Interpersonal relations. | Intimacy (Psychology)
Classification: LCC BF575.A86 B38 2022 (print) |
LCC BF575.A86 (ebook) | DDC 155.6—dc20
LC record available at https://lccn.loc.gov/2022004971
LC ebook record available at https://lccn.loc.gov/2022004972

Printed in Canada
4th Printing

Book design by Laura K. Corless

This is a work of nonfiction. Some names and identifying details have been changed.

To my cosmic partner, Sven.
It is your continuous love that
allows me to feel supported
in ways I never imagined possible.

CONTENTS

Contents

INTRODUCTION

n my young adult years, I was a train wreck when it came to dating. I'd stay in relationships to avoid being alone, and the men I
dated were emotionally unavailable and unattuned to my needs. I
was miserable. I felt rejected by their apparent lack of interest and
angry that they didn't seem to care enough to ask me what I needed.

I want to share two experiences that shook me to my core and
activated my deep-rooted attachment patterns. They touched the
same wounds, but they look very different on the outside. At nineteen, I had a boyfriend who was very wrapped up in work because he
had his own company. After the first rush, when the relationship
became less exciting, he turned his attention back to work, which I
now know is just what he needed to do. He was not a bad guy. He was
just someone starting his own company and under a lot of stress. But
his slow withdrawal touched a place of abandonment inside me and I

began to feel anxious. I lost weight, and life began to feel meaning-less. It scared me, and over time the turmoil inside of me built up to be so intense that I had to be hospitalized for severe anxiety. When the doctor asked me why I was there, I simply said, "Because my boyfriend doesn't love me." My fear of being alone had been just be-low the surface and the shift from intense togetherness to more dis-connection awakened a profound internal unease. I didn't understand what was happening; I felt like I was going insane. I read every book on codependency, and while they helped, it still didn't explain what was happening inside my body.

Years later, I married a man who was unable to stay in connection at all. When we first started dating, I didn't think much of it when he didn't text me back. But over time, I became hypersensitive to even micro-disengagements. A pattern of him pulling away and me reach-ing out for contact happened every six to eight weeks. I felt trapped inside the never-ending cycle but believed that the commitment of marriage would somehow change the dynamic and bring me a sense of security. Now it makes sense to me that as soon as we got closer to intimacy (and I started to feel safe), he would pull away because of his own terror of closeness. He would stop texting, and communication became flat and vague. As he grew more distant, I felt as if no one was on the other side when I looked at him. My whole body would re-spond to seeing him disconnect. Within a microsecond, my heart would race and my gut would fall through the floor, as if something was being ripped out of me. My vision blurred and I felt panic swirl-ing up inside me. When I was unable to get back into connection, I would curl up in a fetal position, feeling just as lost and abandoned as I had when I was very small. His inability to connect, particularly his blank stare, had taken me to a primal experience of abandonment. It was as if my lifeline or oxygen had been cut off.

My early adult years were dark and confusing. I couldn't understand what was happening in my body and emotions, so I felt unhinged. What changed that was learning about my attachment patterns, nervous system responses, and core wounds. I could look back and recognize that the constant feeling of separation anxiety had been with me my whole life. This allowed me to make sense of my physical experience, and created a foundation for compassion and healing. I actually wrote this book to provide you with just that—a deep understanding of what's *really* going on in your body and why you developed in a way that often leads to self-abandonment. With that support, we will take a healing journey together that will provide you with the inner security to make fulfilling relationships possible.

Let's begin with some questions. If you are wondering whether you are anxiously attached, going slowly through this list will provide some insight. These are the feelings and behaviors we experience when our childhood has left us with a lot of legitimate anxiety about whether someone will stay with us or not. Some of them are about the anxiety itself and some are about the ways we try to protect ourselves from that anxiety. Please be gentle with yourself as you go slowly through them.

Do you find yourself continuously thinking about your current partner at the expense of other interests?

Do you constantly talk with your friends about your partner and your relationship?

Do you give up what you want to do in order to do what you believe your partner wants?

Do you initially see your partner through rose-colored glasses and then become disappointed when they don't perfectly meet your needs?

If your partner doesn't answer a text quickly, do you become more anxious?

Do you find yourself making up stories about what it means if your partner doesn't respond quickly?

Do you make repeated attempts to contact your partner when you don't initially get a response?

Do you get attached very quickly and then become anxious about whether the relationship will last?

Do you sometimes threaten to leave when your partner doesn't give you as much attention as you want?

Do you withdraw from your partner when this person doesn't meet your needs for contact?

Do you rush to reestablish connection after a conflict, insisting on continuing the conversation until you feel connected again?

Do you lecture and blame your partner for not staying in contact as much as you need?

Do you keep score of your partner's failures?

Do you get angry easily—either at yourself or at your
partner—if that person isn't available as much as you need?

Do you think about or actually have an affair to make your
partner jealous?

Do you stalk your partner online to know about their
every move?

Do you hack into your partner's phone to see who they are in
contact with and be sure they aren't lying to you?

First of all, know that it is absolutely okay if you identify with
all or some of these behaviors—you will soon start to understand
why you have these tendencies and feel more compassion toward
yourself. It can be painful or feel shaming to look at these emotions
and behaviors head-on. However, the work we will do together will
also open the door to recognizing that you are in pain and fearful,
and deserve support in healing the wounds that drive these ways of
reacting in a relationship.

Let's begin in a place that might sound strange. What if I were
to tell you that to improve the quality of your relationships you need
to focus on yourself more often? It probably goes against everything
you've learned about what it means to be a loving, caring partner.
Maybe you even believe that in order to receive love you must keep
giving, as if love is something that must be earned. But it's the one
piece of guidance I find myself sharing time and again: to cultivate
healthy relationships we need to learn to deeply understand ourselves and heal the wounds that keep us in this miserable cycle, so

we can enter our next partnership feeling stronger and more secure within ourselves. I refer to this transformational process as becoming *self-full*.

When you show up in your relationships from this empowered place, game-playing and attention-seeking tactics have no appeal for you. You will also attract people who are more compatible with you. You will have the skills and balance to work with whatever difficulties come up, and the wisdom to know if or when it's time to leave.

As a practicing couples counselor for more than ten years, I have helped thousands of women and men become more self-full and attract and establish supportive intimate relationships. I do this work because my own healing journey has taught me it is possible to change the way we respond in relationships. The key to this for me was understanding that I was *anxiously attached*, and the patterns were playing out in all my romantic relationships. This relationship style is rooted in deep insecurity and often manifests in a kind of addiction to love. A good indication that we're stuck in this type of relationship is when we know it's hurting us, but we stay trapped in it anyway or keep attracting the same type of relationship, leaving us confused and drained.

It helped so much to learn that early interactions I had as a baby and young child established these energetic patterns in my nervous system that were showing up in my love life. Confronting this meant getting real about the fact that trying to use romantic relationships to "fix" what I felt was broken in me, or to complete me, had only led me deeper into disappointment and misery. I needed to slow down, gather trustworthy support around me, and spend time healing the anxiety that my parents, with all good intentions, had hardwired inside me.

This isn't about blaming our parents for anything. They did the best they could with what they received. And they most likely loved us the way they knew how, but love isn't all that is needed to build a rock-solid foundation for a secure sense of self. It requires parents who can see and be fully present for us as we are, even when we are messy, angry, or sad. They also need to be loving and curious about who we are becoming by supporting all aspects of our selves. Because they are really seeing us, they are good at reflecting our inner state to us and are equipped to repair the mistakes they might have made. All of this creates safety for us to grow into our authentic self with confidence. These experiences with our parents are literally building our brains in ways that will support us being able to have relationships that feel just this fulfilling when we're ready for friendship and then romance. Perhaps most important is that we are also internalizing them as ongoing companions who form the core of an inner community that will nurture us throughout our lives. We'll be exploring more about the brain and about internalization later in this book.

Many parents simply didn't get what they needed to be able to provide this kind of safety for us. When we internalize them, we also take in their anxiety or anger or absence. Then it's up to us to get serious about the repair work. I have to say this process of healing was the most difficult thing I have ever done. It meant revisiting past wounds, which bit by bit allowed my deep-rooted expectations about how relationships feel to change. The biggest catalyst for doing this work was the end of my first marriage. I faced a lot of loneliness, confusion, and fear as I challenged myself to be okay with being single. What I didn't realize is that the relationship was uncovering my deep subconscious wounds so I could heal them. During this time, I started to seek emotionally present friendships, leaning on the friends who were warm and consistent. This helped me feel supported while I worked on repairing my inner world. Their care gave me the safety I needed to do the work and also helped to calm my nervous system. I know that I internalized them because I can feel their kindhearted support like a community as I write this. And slowly, as I healed, I didn't lose myself in romantic love the way I had. This process has led to a sense of inner calm, stability, awareness of my needs, and trust in myself that I never imagined was possible. Eventually, it led me to a loving partner with whom I have formed a more secure attachment. In the container of this new relationship, I began to integrate all my growth and newfound awareness, allowing us to reach deeper layers of truly fulfilling intimacy. As a result, I feel supported by him in a way I never knew existed—and I'm able to show him the same level of steady support and acceptance in return. Regardless of where you are on your journey, the transformation process we will explore together in this book will allow you, too, to understand what you need to heal old wounds so that you can cultivate healthy, loving, and sustainable relationships. I wrote this book because this is my wish for you.

In the first three chapters, we will focus on deepening our understanding of our selves and our behaviors in relationships. This will allow us to develop wisdom and compassion for the parts of our selves that we may have wanted to disown. This awareness and acceptance becomes the foundation for change.

We'll begin by looking at two attachment styles, each developed in childhood, that leave people with different patterns of relating as adults, especially in their closest relationships. Some people have developed an anxious attachment style like the one I described in myself. This is different than the feelings we all have at the beginning of a new relationship. Because everything is new and unknown, the dynamics don't always surface in the beginning. Each person is going through a lot of different feelings, and it makes sense that at times we are *all* left questioning if it's really safe to let go and be vulnerable. It can be confusing because the relationship can start out feeling blissful and exciting until intimacy fears surface and our core wounds are activated, leaving us feeling lost and bewildered.

Anxious attachment stems from a deep sense of *inner instability* where old wounds make people anticipate that they will be abandoned again and again. These feelings can result in behavior that—ironically—only pushes a partner further away: texting dozens of times in a row, hacking his or her phone, obsessing over social media posts, or becoming clingy and jealous. Underneath all those behaviors are feelings of terror and a desperate need to keep this person close and attentive. The result? Turbulent, painful, and ultimately unsustainable relationships.

This book is written for those with anxious attachment, but it will also be helpful to understand the style at the other end of the spectrum. Avoidant attachment is also rooted in early childhood experiences with parents who weren't present for us or able to offer enough emotional support, but avoidants developed a different coping mechanism. Seeing that it was dangerous to depend on others in a relationship, avoidant types learned to protect themselves by staying distant from intimacy. They are often dedicated to their careers and tend to back away when closeness threatens. Criticism of their partners can give them reasons for ending the relationship. While this is not my style of attaching, I have had lots of experience being on the receiving end. We focus on these two because they are often attracted to each other like a moth to a flame.

In the next chapter, we'll explore the world of the youngest parts of our selves, referring to this part of us as *Little Me*, who learned what they had to do to keep parents in connection with us. Compassion tends to blossom when we get a real taste of how the behaviors we may dislike the most in ourselves were absolutely essential for staying attached to those who were most central in our lives. These early losses lead to core wounds that we may not be consciously aware of, but drive us to continue the patterns as we grow into adulthood.

With this understanding, in the last chapter in part one, we can explore how the anxious-avoidant dance of adult relationships emerges from these childhood experiences. Two people seeking a loving relationship get drawn into familiar patterns of protection because of the core wounds of childhood. This leads to what Melody Beattie calls a codependent relationship. A very short definition of codependency is trying to control another person's emotions and behaviors so we don't have to experience our own painful feelings. *If I can get you to stay close to me, I won't have to feel the frightening abandonment that is lurking inside me* (anxious person). *If I can stay far enough away from you, I won't have to experience the vulnerability that threatens to make me feel the black hole of emptiness inside me* (avoidant person). Each person is actually depending on the other to provide protection, but in ways that guarantee more misery for both people. Avoidant people become even more convinced that relationships are to be avoided, and anxious people, who are more in touch with their emotions, suffer agonizing abandonment as they become selfless in the attempt to keep the other person. This is a dynamic we'll be exploring in depth.

In the last part of this chapter, we will touch on the kind of wounds that lead to the even more destructive behaviors of love addiction for the anxious person and narcissistic self-focus for the avoidant person. Having experienced this kind of relationship myself, I know the pain of it and the necessity of healing the wounds that make those of us who are anxiously attached vulnerable.

Then we will move into the heart of the book, the work of healing the core wounds and becoming self-full. We'll walk through all of it together. Perhaps the most important lesson I learned in addressing my own anxious attachment style is that facing my deepest fears of abandonment, loneliness, and not being worthy of love is the key to becoming healthily self-full and ready for a balanced relationship. The longer we ignore these vulnerable, wounded parts of our selves, the longer we'll have the heartbreaking experience of being in relationships that feel just like the abandonment and fear that was a familiar feeling from childhood.

As human beings, we have a hard time with pain, often doing everything we can to avoid the discomfort of facing the ache inside us. The inner work of becoming self-full, which includes locating exactly where it hurts and attending with kindness to these hurting parts, is no exception, to the extent that many of us will go our whole lives without addressing our pain. Even when we instinctively sense that this is how we free ourselves of unhealthy attachments, we often shy away because we don't have the necessary support to get in touch with this deeper pain and fear. Our society often encourages us to go through this alone, but it's important to find the right people, in the form of a therapist or one or two friends who can listen with warmth and without judgment. I will also have the privilege of holding your hand throughout this book. I will be working with you to help you develop your new internal support system. Allowing yourself to feel cared for and listened to by others will also create a sense of safety, which is the vital and often missing ingredient to becoming self-full. This external safety net will soothe your nervous system, build an inner community of care, and allow you to be fully embodied and gain the awareness to respond differently to your attachment needs when they arise. Over time, you will find yourself feeling so much more secure.

We'll begin with a reflective practice that will help us build what is called *interoception*. This means listening to our body's sensations to bring us into contact with our inner world. This is the place where our core wounds have been protectively stored until someone comes to support us in healing. We can be with our younger self, our Little Me, hold their experiences, and meet our Inner Protectors and Inner Nurturers. Because you and I are holding this space together, and you will also be seeking other companions— a therapist or trustworthy friends—you will have what you need for this part of the journey.

Having started to develop the capacity to listen inside, in the next chapter, your Little Me will begin their healing journey. You can return here again and again for the guided practices that will give them the support they need for the rest of your life. To accompany you, I am recording these meditations so we can do them together. This part of the journey will be painful at times as we touch the fear and anguish that has been hurting inside since you were small. What makes it possible is the care and warmth we bring with our listening presence while building internal resources that will last a lifetime. This movement toward becoming self-full becomes possible because you are brave enough to do this work.

In the last chapter in part two, we will explore the movement from selfless to self-full. What you can expect when you emerge from this journey. We will spend a little time reviewing where we've been and then celebrate the new fullness that is emerging as we continue to support Little Me's recovery and build a strong Inner Nurturer community. There is a guided practice for strengthening self-fullness along with a growing sense of gratitude for this new solid ground.

Now we're ready for part three. What will it be like to move toward interdependence with a partner? In this kind of relationship, both partners have enough inner security to not depend on only each other for connection and also to be at ease with growing intimacy. At the same time, they can lean into each other to provide support. We could say that they neither abandon nor invade each other. Weaving this new way of being into a partnership is challenging and rewarding. It means developing new kinds of internal and external boundaries (chapter 7), gaining skill in working through the hard parts so that the repair work between two people strengthens rather than disrupts the relationship (chapter 8), and drawing on the universe's resources to sustain a life that is ever-renewing its capacity to manifest love (chapter 9).

I believe that people come into our lives for a reason, and that each person we cross paths with has a valuable lesson to share with us. We just need to be open to receive it. Seen this way, we might say that the underlying nature of all relationships is spiritual. This is why the path to becoming self-full is also a spiritual journey toward wholeness, one in which we seek to establish a connection, not only to our inner selves, but to a source of unconditional love and support that's greater than anything we can put into words.

There is a profound mystery in this journey inward. We may begin to feel that we are divinely supported, never alone, and that the universe really does have our backs. Relational neuroscience also tells us that we are built for these kinds of safe and nurturing connections that fill our bodies with the neurochemicals of warm, secure bonds. Trusting in this spiritual connection and the right human support, we begin to act more spontaneously and creatively, increasing our chances of fulfilling love to make its way in. As you begin to heal, you will feel more secure in the world, within your relationships, and within yourself.

I share this as motivation for the journey we are about to begin, a journey to better understand and heal your hurts, so you no longer need to seek outside for *all* your comfort and nurturing. The work in these pages—which includes guided meditations and practices to help you navigate through your deepest emotional wounds and needs—is designed to illuminate parts of your inner world that require TLC, while encouraging you to explore how the dynamics of past relationships were actually shining a light on these sore, vulnerable parts all along. As you move through this book, please go at your own pace and honor the time it takes to move deeply into your inner world. We can do this together.

1

How We Lose
Ourselves

CHAPTER 1

The Role of Relationships

The first and most important thing I want you to know is that your desire to be in a relationship is the most natural thing in the world. We are all hardwired to connect with others on an intimate level. We are born physically connected to our mother by the umbilical cord that has literally been our only source of sustenance, the magical thread of life itself. As babies and young children, we continue to rely on our parents and wider family group to survive, while part of growing up means learning to become more self-sufficient, until eventually, we are capable of meeting our own survival needs. As we grow into adulthood, our society tells us it is important to be self-reliant and independent, but if we are anxiously attached, our inner world tells us that we must cling close in relationships or we will be abandoned. In truth, the blueprint for the middle way, for interdependence, is inked before we even take our first breath. We are social creatures from birth until our last moment, always reaching for safe people we can lean into who can also lean into us. Nothing says "I am safe" like truly connecting with another person.

Once we find ourselves out in the world, seeking connection outside of our immediate family, how do we know the person we are trusting with our feelings is up to the job and isn't going to take our tender, open heart and trample on it? Faced with this uncertainty, as adults we tend to stifle our desire to connect by becoming hyper-independent, or else we burn through one relationship after another, as a quick fix for the ache of loneliness inside. While it's true that we no longer need the kinds of connections that ensure we will be fed, clothed, and sheltered, our adult relationships fulfill two different—but equally important—roles: the need to see and know ourselves through the eyes of another in a way that allows us to feel supported and safe, and the satisfaction of long-term intimacy with another.

In our most intimate relationships, the ones where we feel truly safe and relaxed enough to be our "real" selves, we are able to access even deeper states of being and discover the joy of being accepted for who we truly are. In this way, our close relationships become a mirror in which to meet our *whole* selves. Secure in this whole self, we can understand our deepest needs and seek to have them met as we confidently stake out our place in the world. Nothing is more validating and freeing than the permission to simply be *us*—and in a healthy relationship, this permission is granted on both sides in an ongoing, unconditional mutual exchange of acceptance and appreciation. When this is the case, conflicts are seen as a way to build the empathy and understanding that can bring us even closer together. This all helps us to feel comfortable with intimacy, allowing us to give and receive love more easily.

Depending on the influences of our parental and cultural upbringing, we can struggle to form these secure and healthy attachments. Perhaps as children we experienced a sense of disinterest in us, so we learned how to cope on our own. Or maybe we were only intermittently attended to, so we anxiously cling to any scraps of attention and affection that come our way, not trusting that there will always be enough. When the foundation for our connections has been built on shaky ground, we must heal these core wounds so we can create the secure relationships we desire.

WHAT IS ATTACHMENT THEORY?

Attachment theory, also known as the science of how we connect in early childhood, was pioneered by the psychologist John Bowlby in the 1950s. Bowlby explained that, as babies, we are dependent on caregivers for our basic needs, and the way those caregivers (our parents, grandparents, and siblings) tend to our needs creates an *attachment style*. This can affect the way we relate with others throughout childhood and into adulthood. Bowlby, along with his colleague Mary Ainsworth, also identified three different attachment styles: anxious, avoidant, and secure. An understanding of these relational patterns forms the basis of my work as a couples therapist—and also helped me understand my own relationship tendencies after my first marriage ended in a devastating divorce. At an emotional rock bottom, I knew the time had come for me to make a change. I realized I needed to forge an inner sense of security that had been lacking all my life as I discovered that my own anxious attachment style was at the heart of my unhappiness.

As I described in the introduction, those who experienced being anxiously attached are frightened of being abandoned because their parents were so inconsistent in providing connection. To protect themselves from this happening again, they tend to focus all their energy on finding a relationship. Their need to maintain the connection often emotionally suffocates their partners because they can't stop themselves from obsessing over their partners' level of commitment. When this new person begins to pull back, feelings of not deserving love often come to the surface. Their lives can become an endless search for a relationship that will prove they are lovable, but the need to cling for reassurance out of fear and insecurity creates demands that often lead to the very abandonment they fear.

Meanwhile, people with avoidant attachment have a strong need to hit the eject button at the first sign of intimacy. In this case, the core belief is the same—*I will not receive the love I need*, but it was delivered differently by parents who were consistently unable to provide for the emotional needs of their children. Their natural conclusion is that they have to go it alone, so they learn to prize their independence and self-sufficiency above all else because they don't believe anyone will provide for their emotional needs.

Those who are securely attached are more comfortable with intimacy and trust that their emotional needs will be met. As children, their parents consistently offered warmth and care, communicating how lovable they were. This primes them to expect and want interdependency in their adult relationships. They are able to offer their love and support to a partner without losing their sense of self, so they can easily transition from a feeling of being closely connected to more on their own without becoming afraid that the relationship is ending.

Many of us have experienced more than one attachment style as children. Maybe our mother was anxious and inconsistent and our father was often silent behind his newspaper. Since we have both those patterns inside us, either of them can come up depending on who we're in a relationship with now. If we're feeling a friend or partner is clinging to us, the avoidance we experienced with our father may activate us to pull away. If we're with someone who has a tendency to pull away, we may find the anxiety we experienced with our mother rushing to the surface. As we move through this work together, you will get greater clarity about your own tendencies, patterns, and needs in different situations. This will gradually help you have a better understanding of what you need in a romantic partner.

People who have had a secure upbringing often wonder why they still have insecure feelings at times. It is important to realize that all of us can still have anxiety when our partners have a strong tendency to pull away from intimacy. Those feelings are an adaptive early warning system telling you to be more aware of what is happening between the two of you. Having this knowledge in your emotional tool kit will remind you that attachment is always a two-person experience.

Neither of these attachment styles is "better" than the other. The way we are in relationships is part of what makes us who we are. Whether anxious, avoidant, or secure, our way of connecting with others has developed over the course of our lifetime as we adapt the best way we can to conditions in our family. Rather than something that needs to be changed overnight, the real strength lies in learning to understand and work *with* the unique needs of our attachment type while we are healing, so that we can focus on relationships that allow us to thrive *exactly as we are*.

In this book, we will be looking mainly at the anxious attachment style, the one I'm guessing you most identify with, since the book's title must have resonated with you. You've probably nursed a broken heart time and again as you question why you keep attracting partners who seem hyper-independent or so narcissistic that they are seemingly unable to understand you, let alone meet your emotional needs. For your part, you perceive relationships differently, believing that in order to love and be loved, you must give everything you've got, and then some. That it is virtuous to be *selfless* in your relationships. As compelling as this may feel, it is actually the fast track to losing ourselves in love, which may sound romantic but is the opposite of the grounded path to self-discovery and self-acceptance that is the real role of our intimate adult relationships.

The theory of adult romantic attachment was originally formulated by psychologists Cindy Hazan and Phillip R. Shaver in the 1980s. Their groundbreaking research showed that up to fifty-six percent of people have a secure attachment style, while twenty-five percent are anxiously attached, and nineteen percent are avoidant. These proportions have changed some over the following decades, with secure attachments becoming fewer while insecure ones are on the rise, probably because of the increasing stress of daily life. Hazan and Shaver also noticed that our earliest attachment experiences strongly influence how we come into adult relationships, particularly the most intimate ones. The closer the relationship, the more it stimulates our earlier expectations about attachment.

Their research also suggested that particular kinds of attachment styles may be attracted to each other. As I mentioned in the introduction, anxious and avoidant people are often drawn to each other. The avoidant person may feel attracted to the anxious person because they crave the very thing the avoidant person is so desperate to avoid: intimacy. Meanwhile, the anxious person is hypervigilant in their quest for stability, something that the avoidant person is unlikely to be able to provide. Let's take a closer look at how this plays out, using my relationship with my ex-husband as an example.

When we first met, everything was wonderful between us. He was very thoughtful and would plan lots of fun dates for us. Best of all, his attention was consistent. He even seemed to express his emotions openly and freely, telling me he loved me without hesitation. But the closer and more intimate we became, the more *our individual fears about relationships* kicked in. This manifested differently for both of us, according to our attachment styles. As he would feel fear, he would pull back and I would run toward him for comfort and reassurance. The more my anxiety made me want to reach out to him, the more his avoidance was pulling him back. When I felt him withdraw, I would panic and try for his attention even more, texting multiple times in a row, for example. Being avoidant, he would feel threatened by both my neediness and the expression of my emotions, shut down emotionally, and cut off all contact. Then he would break up with me. As time passed, he would feel less pressured and remember how much he loved me. He'd come back to me one hundred and fifty percent committed. But as soon as things got back to normal, the dance would begin all over again.

I'm sure you can relate to this scenario. It's a familiar cycle for most people with anxious attachment. We are driven by so much fear that we will do whatever we need to do to hold on to a relationship at any cost. You've probably heard people say, "I want a man to take care of me." Or "Everything will be fine once I get married." And while it's true that a healthy relationship can help us become the best version of ourselves, the clue is in the phrasing of these statements, which suggests that a romantic partner will be the solution to all our problems. When we think this way, the desire to find a mate becomes a desperate search for something we perceive as lacking in our own being. Rather than seeing our relationships as a crucible in which to better understand ourselves (while sharing fulfilling intimacy), we reach for a partner to complete us.

When we do this, we begin tapping into an energy source, our partners' energy, instead of our own, to the point where we can't function without their love and attention. Rather than relying on our own inner resources in times of need, we turn to our partners to make us feel whole again. And this may actually work for a while. We begin to feel more secure, while at the same time beginning to touch into the fears of losing this security, and we tell ourselves, "This is who I've been searching for." Those sensations are rapidly followed by "If he leaves me, I won't survive. I have to hold on to him." To prevent this loss, we are likely to abandon ourselves completely while putting the needs of our partners above our own, hoping to make them rely on *us* the way we have come to rely on *them*.

Take Sam, a client of mine who seemed to function rather well on her own. She worked in PR and had a vibrant social life. She started dating Mark, who was the kind of man she always dreamed about. Great looking, great job, attentive, and fun. She fell fast and hard. He did all the right things, too. He took her to fancy restaurants, texted her throughout the day, was nice to her family, and even talked about their future life as a couple. They did everything together. Sam stopped going to her workout classes, waiting for him to make their plans. She started missing "girls' nights" and her weekend visits with her sister. I could see that Sam was becoming deeply attached to Mark and was giving up so many wonderful parts of her life. She started to devote all her energies to tending to his every need. After a few months, she was one hundred percent sure that he was the one. And that's when he started to pull away. He stopped checking in with her during the day, started spending much of the weekend with the guys, and wouldn't explain what changed when she questioned him. Also, Mark might not have been able to tell her why he was pulling away since her clinging was waking up his early childhood experience, likely without him even being aware.

I saw her slowly unravel. She couldn't understand what was happening, saying things like, "I changed my whole life for him. I thought he was going to propose. I don't know what to do without him." Mark saw her become unglued, and so he became more withdrawn. It was heartbreaking to watch as Sam went into a downward spiral. She stopped being a top performer at her job. Her group of friends and her family, who were initially happy for her, were now very hurt and felt used because she had neglected them during her time with Mark. Her confidence took a hit. She started to grow more and more anxious and unsure of herself. Mark eventually broke it off for good. Sam and I had some serious inner work to do together.

Looking back, there was a constant hum of anxiety in the backdrop of this relationship. For Sam, this urgent need for connection is one of the symptoms of an attachment system that was met with anxiety and unpredictability rather than with consistent nurturing as an infant, toddler, and beyond. It left Sam with a nervous system that tracked the safety and availability of whomever she had currently chosen as the primary caretaker of her needs. In this case, Mark. Those who are anxiously attached tend to have a hypersensitive attachment system that makes them place their availability to their partner first as a default setting and push all their other needs and priorities to the back burner.

This makes a great deal of sense. If growing up you had inconsistency in your primary attachments, as an adult you spend your life waiting for the other shoe to drop when it comes to relationships. You are appropriately vigilant and sensitive, given what you learned as a child. As a result, you're always on high alert, looking for subtle changes in your partner's mood, constantly watching for indications that something is wrong, so you lose your sense of safety and your body goes into a state of physical distress at the first sign of abandonment. If you are someone with a secure attachment style, when your partner doesn't text you back immediately, you might think, "He must be busy at work." But if you have anxious attachment, you quickly turn to the thought, "He isn't that into me." Or "Something is wrong with us." Again, this makes sense because your earliest learning was that relationships were not reliable.

Remember how I described the feeling of my former husband pulling away? *My gut would fall through the floor, as if something was being ripped out of me.* Since our second brain, the one in our belly, is concerned with safety, this dramatic feeling was telling me that I felt in great danger of being abandoned. When we feel this way, rational thinking goes out the window and the protective fight-or-flight survival state kicks in, and the behaviors that we think will help us stay in connection start to play out. These can be things like incessant texting, apologizing for things that weren't our fault, even stalking, anything to fix the issue and reestablish connection. Once, I even got in my car and drove by my ex's house, trying to track him down when he wasn't answering my texts. From one viewpoint, that might seem completely irrational, but from the perspective of my earliest experiences and fears around abandonment, these behaviors all made perfect sense. It was also a surefire way to push him further away from me. But my hair-trigger attachment system was simply doing whatever it could to help me feel safe.

HARDWIRED FOR CONNECTION

Ideally, the role of our relationships is to help us feel okay to be the person we already are, but an activated anxious attachment style creates a feeling of uneasiness in our whole body. The extreme physical reaction I experienced anytime my ex pulled away from me made me feel like I was going insane, but I learned that this was just the way my nervous system had been primed to react when I experienced disconnection or detachment from my partner. Gaining an understanding of the workings of the *autonomic nervous system* (ANS) allowed me to get this level of self-compassion. Dr. Stephen Porges, the scientist who developed something called the *polyvagal theory*, can offer us this kind of clarity. According to Porges, "Connection is a biological imperative"—which means we are neurobiologically as well as psychologically hardwired for connection. Let me explain why this is so important to understand.

It's the job of the ANS to keep us in a state of connection in order to keep us safe. Over the course of our evolution, where our survival as humans has relied on us being accepted as part of our tribe or group, three branches of the ANS have developed—these "wandering nerves" give us three differing responses to cues in our internal and external worlds. Porges coined the term *neuroception* to describe this process, which is essentially how our system becomes aware of whether or not we feel safe. This process operates like a radar that's constantly scanning our environment as our system subconsciously asks, "Are you with me?" Meaning: Are you nonjudgmentally receptive to me just as I am in this moment? Do you really see me? Have you got my back? If we have a falling-out, will you turn against me?

When this radar detects that we are safe, the branch of the ANS that allows us to warmly attach to others is activated. This creates what's called the *ventral state*. It helps us listen to one another, softens the quality of our voices, relaxes the muscles around our eyes, and makes our faces mobile and expressive, so we can better communicate our emotions. Beyond words, these physical changes signal to other people that it is safe to approach, open up, and engage. We can't fake this state. It only happens when we feel safe in the presence of others—which means that when we feel threatened, the opposite is true: The ventral state shuts down, and it is not possible to connect.

This is what I experienced anytime my ex-husband would pull away. Sensing that I was being abandoned, another branch of the ANS would be activated, putting me in a state known as *sympathetic arousal*. Designed to protect me from any external threat to my safety, this activated state is commonly referred to as the *fight-or-flight response*. Our ears begin to scan for danger, so we can no longer hear the subtle meaning of what people are saying. The area around our eyes tightens. Our gaze sharpens. Our voice takes on a particular intonation that signals danger. In the context of my relationship, this is what led to the constant texting, the chasing, and my doing whatever I could to get his attention. Even worse, when we go into a state of sympathetic arousal, it can trigger a similar response in others. Our human nervous systems are extremely sensitive and are designed to resonate with those around us, so as I began to telegraph danger to my partner, he adaptively moved into fight-or-flight as well. And while my tendency was to mobilize my energies to "fight," taking actions to try to keep him close, his learned response was to "flee."

Now, there's also a third branch of the ANS that only comes into play when we feel so helpless and so terrified that we feel like our life is threatened. Imagine a baby crying and crying in her crib with no one coming. She is in sympathetic arousal, calling for help. After a while, she becomes quiet. She has given up hope that help will arrive—triggering the *dorsal* branch of the ANS. In an attempt to minimize energetic output in the face of perceived extreme danger, everything in our system slows down, including our breathing and heart rate. Our faces become pale and we begin to disconnect from the world around us, making ourselves as small and "invisible" as possible. This disappearance is a kind of hibernation in the face of helplessness that lets us hold on to our resources for a better day. For example, there were times in my relationship when I felt so ashamed about getting emotional that I wanted to have no feelings at all. I have come to understand that this feeling of wanting to shut down and hide was a result of my own dorsal response kicking in because I'd given up on getting my partner to respond, just like the baby crying in her crib would eventually exhaust herself and shut down. Below is an illustration to show all three branches of the ANS, and how this information highway runs through our body.

What's interesting is that all of these ANS responses are adaptive to what's happening in both our outer *and* inner worlds. While on the outside, my ex was taking actions that triggered a fearful sympathetic reaction, this was also a response to my inner state—the experiences of my early life having led to the subconscious core belief that others would always pull away when I needed them. Powerful physical sensations are what drove me to take the actions I did, just as my partner's early experiences were causing him to pull further away.

So, is it possible to get the ANS to override these responses? Yes and no. The ANS begins to develop along with the rest of our neural pathways in the womb. About three months after we are con-

Autonomic Nervous System
(ANS)

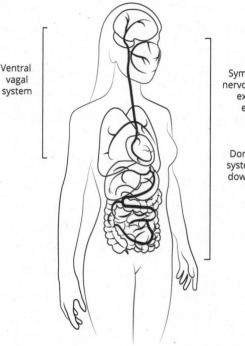

Ventral
vagal
system

Sympathetic
nervous system
expands
energy

+

Dorsal vagal
system shuts
down energy

ceived, our system begins to parallel our mother's. If she is relaxed and content during her pregnancy, our developing ANS will pick up on this. Before we are even born, we begin to learn that the world is a safe and benevolent place. However, if she is regularly anxious, our nervous system and neurochemicals will begin to match hers, and we come into the world primed for fear. After we are born, we meet our mother face-to-face, and so begins what Deb Dana (another writer on polyvagal theory) calls the "dyadic dance of connection."

Regardless of the feeling tone of our mother's pregnancy, we are all born expecting to be warmly received by this person who has carried and nurtured us in the earliest stages of our existence. Our mother (or primary caregiver) is also the first person that we attempt to connect with—which we do by seeking *co-regulation* with her. For example, anytime we're upset or hungry, if she is attentive to what we need, then more often than not she will provide us with comfort or food. This teaches us that when we express them, our needs will be met. Because we calm when she attends to us, our mother also experiences warm feelings. Mother and baby dancing together. Meanwhile, on an emotional level, our mother being curious and interested in who this new little person is reflects to us that our existence matters.

Ideally, this co-regulation happens through an instinctive and unspoken connection with our mother and other primary caregivers. In an ideal world, they are intuitively attuned to our needs even when we have a limited repertoire as babies and young toddlers—crying or throwing a tantrum. These early experiences of dependable safety and connection put us in the ventral state, helping us trust that we will also be warmly received and cared for by others. Meanwhile, when co-regulation occurs, two processes are happening in our neural system: the actual connections between neurons that allow us to regulate our emotions are developing, and we are internalizing our mother's loving presence as a *constant inner companion*. As we grow older and gradually become more independent, a natural part of our development, both of these processes are what help us feel "okay" even when there is no one on the outside taking care of us in the moment.

It's probably not a surprise to learn that my early life did not build this kind of circuitry, as is the case for many of those who are anxiously attached. The mother I internalized was anxious, depressed, and full of fear. Not only did she experience postpartum depression after I was born, but she also shared that she was constantly worried about me. In addition, her attention was sometimes drawn away from me because she was also deeply unhappy in her marriage. Since my mother was struggling herself and locked into her own sympathetic and dorsal ANS responses, she was unable to provide steady attunement. As a result, my nervous system began to expect for my needs *not* to be met, for people to only be present part of the time, and for them to unexpectedly break off the connection. My mom's personal struggles and lack of support impacted her ability to consistently co-regulate with me also meant that I didn't build the circuitry that would help me quiet my own nervous system as an adult, while I also internalized a parent who only stoked my anxiety. In addition, my father was struggling with depression and substance abuse, which made him unavailable, and I internalized that absence. When babies' natural outreach toward their caregivers goes unmet, they also develop a *felt sense*, which is the feelings, sensations, and a bodily knowing that there is *something wrong with them*. As a result, many of us, myself included, enter our adult relationships with this sensation of "wrongness" tucked deep inside and out of sight—until we find ourselves moving toward intimacy and there is no more hiding it.

Learning all of this helped me see that my out-of-control feelings, sensations, and behaviors with my former husband were the result of wiring that developed when I was very young. My brain wasn't making a conscious choice to feel or act this way; it was simply responding to signals that my nervous system perceived as a threat. Even more challenging, these responses happen at lightning speed while the rest of our brain operates at a much slower pace— and once the alarm in our body senses this painful disconnection, our conscious thoughts can't stop it. However, it *is* possible to rewire our ability to regulate—the missing link in our developmental process as infants who did not receive consistent caregiving. Thanks to something called *neuroplasticity*, our brains can develop new circuitry *at any age*. The process of becoming self-full involves having the experiences of care and soothing we needed as children now. We will be going through this process together in these pages, as we draw on positive experiences from your past to create a new internalized intuitively nurturing parent. In addition, you will also learn the importance of connecting with available supportive people in your life today. As a result, you will begin to feel a sense of safety inside your own body that you may never have experienced before. This in turn will help you stay in the ventral state of connection for longer even in the midst of experiences that would have once sent you over the edge. More and more, you will be able to respond consciously when big feelings are activated in your relationships rather than reacting from a sympathetic state.

Over time, and with practice, the new connections in your nervous system will strengthen so that even when you feel yourself going into sympathetic arousal, a part of you will be able to simply *observe* your rapid heartbeat or your tightening belly. Developing the ability to notice and understand the meaning of these physical sensations—versus acting on them—is a sign that new neural pathways are forming. You may also find that your ANS returns to a state of equilibrium more quickly and easily than before. This is another surefire sign that rewiring is happening. Eventually, you will even find that your thoughts mirror the changes in your nervous system. Instead of being in a constant state of hypervigilance for the next perceived threat, you will find yourself imagining your partner simply being busy at work when he doesn't return your text—versus it being a sign he is about to break up with you. Eventually, a lack of self-worth will also give way to an innate sense of your own lovability, along with compassion for the protections you developed as a child. Soon, you will find yourself showing up for yourself (and others) in ways that you never imagined could be possible.

THE FAIRY-TALE MYTH

We are fed so many fantasies about romantic love. It begins with the story that our partner is solely responsible for making us feel safe and loved. As a psychotherapist, I assist couples and individuals working through interpersonal hardships. But many of my clients don't actually come to me looking for truly fulfilling love—the kind of healthy, interdependent relationships that will help them grow personally and as a couple. No. They typically show up on my couch looking for a fairy-tale romance with a happily-ever-after resolution, like the ones they've seen in the movies. And while it is possible to find true happiness in an intimate relationship, it is crucial to understand that this happiness *together* primarily comes from first gaining intimacy with *ourselves* and developing a new sense of what loving relationships really feel like.

But, of course, we've been taught the opposite. From Disney princesses being brought to life with a kiss, all the way through the drama of who will invite us to the high-school prom, to countless rom-coms that tell us about the search for the heroine's one perfect love, we are imprinted with the idea that a romantic relationship will somehow save us from a fearful, lonely life. If you have an anxious attachment style, the idea that "I'm lucky to have him" can also result in clinging to the first relationship that comes along, regardless of whether it's right for you or not. My work in cases such as this is to help my clients look honestly at their relationships to see if they have subscribed to the fantasy that their partner is there to save them and, in doing so, have lost their connection to and trust in themselves. Together, we build an understanding that in first coming to accept themselves—to become self-full—their relationships will have a much better chance to mature into a fulfilling interdependency.

We have also been led to believe that marriage—representing the ultimate in commitment—is proof of a partner's love. Beyond the hope that it will bring us happiness and material and emotional security (which is never guaranteed), it's important to look at what marriage actually is—a legal union of two people that has little or no bearing whatsoever on the actual quality of their relationship. There's nothing wrong with wanting to marry the person you love. It can be one of life's most fulfilling experiences. However, I believe that as a society we tend to put too much emphasis on marriage as the ultimate goal or the solution to our problems. In fact, outsourcing our sense of security to another person via a legal contract can be a barrier to us going within ourselves to do the real work of establishing our own sense of safety and stability.

Often, years after the wedding, a client will come into my office and tell me why she *really* decided to get married. Many tell me they got married because they wanted to have a child. Others say they were "getting older" and felt it was now or never. Some admit that they actually knew it wasn't feeling right, like when the prenuptial agreement raised uncomfortable issues, but it was too late—the wedding invitations were sent, and they couldn't pull back. Factors like these lead many people to jump into marriage with a deep sense that it may not be for the right reasons. Often in hindsight, clients admit to all the red flags they saw, as well as how their intuition was actually sending them strong messages that this union wasn't feeling right. Later, these issues that had been ignored showed up in full force as the marriage buckled—leaving both parties feeling like the loneliest souls on the planet.

Another common belief is that marriage is the key to lifelong love. Besides the fact that close to fifty percent of marriages end in divorce, we must realize that not all relationships are supposed to last forever. The majority of our relationships, including our close friendships, are meant to teach us valuable lessons about ourselves so that we can continue to grow and evolve as individuals. Seen this way, any need to be certain about how things will play out becomes less concerning. It's more important to be in the moment with each other and to truly honor the gifts each person brings.

What if, instead of a ring and a proposal, the quality of a

relationship is measured by the growth you both experience within the union and how you grow as a couple? This happens when you feel safe enough with that person to be on your own at times, connecting to your inner and social resources, and then return with new energy to bring into the relationship. I propose this as an alternative to seeking everything from *within* your partnership, which is a symptom of love addiction and a cause of codependency (which we will dive into fully in chapter 3). Wouldn't it be great if society also celebrated this self-full vision of romantic love?

When two people have found a sense of "home" within themselves and have come to terms with who they are, accepting their flaws and understanding their needs, they can begin to build an external home together. At this point, legal marriage vows (not to mention the ring and the dress) are merely the buttercream icing on the three-tiered wedding cake. When you are in a naturally committed relationship, based on a mutual desire to support each other's growth and develop interdependency, marriage becomes less of a destination and more of a progression. You will also feel the relief of growing with someone in a safe and sustainable way. The sense of safety and mutual acceptance behind the marriage agreement are more important than the agreement itself.

ANXIETY AND THE GIFT OF EMPATHY

When we fall in love, we're supposed to sync up with our partner and become one synergistic unit, right? To an extent, yes. In intimate relationships, we are connected to our partner with an energetic cord and with what are called *mirror neurons*, which means that the feelings, moods, thoughts, fears, and actions of each individual are shared. While these originate within one partner, the other is able to sense them. For example, we might feel stressed when our husband is nervous about his job, or get a fit of giggles when our partner starts to laugh. This is a natural function of our ability to feel empathy, an important way we are connected with each other emotionally. These circuits for resonating with others are often highly developed in those with an anxious attachment style because we had to spend so much time and energy tracking parents who weren't able to stay consistently connected to us.

Empathy can be simply defined as an ability to feel what others are feeling, to the point that we can pick up on, and even feel, the energy, moods, and thoughts of others. It can be a blessing to be this sensitive. It's how we connect, how we nurture, and what makes us a good friend. Being empathetic gives us compassion, and helps others feel seen, understood, and that they are not alone. In fact, it's what makes me a caring therapist! But it can become a burden if it is not harnessed. Without proper boundaries, it's possible to lose sight of which feelings are ours and which belong to our partner. We can become so absorbed that we lose track of our feelings entirely.

Anxiously attached children become more sensitive to others so they can feel connected as much as possible. Being hyperaware of the feelings of our parents was a part of the way we adapted to their inconsistency. It makes perfect sense that when we attach to new people as adults, we respond in the ways we learned as children. Being able to gauge the emotional state of our spouse or partner becomes a way to protect against abandonment. While becoming self-full does not mean closing down our capacity for sensitivity or empathy, it is about learning to take care of and listen to our needs also, so we are able to give from a place of wholeness.

When we come to a relationship from a place of insecurity and fear, it's easy to become overwhelmed with a desire to know everything about the person we are falling in love with. Is he happy? What does she need? Does he mean it when he says he loves me? Or is she about to walk out the door? Flooded with information about what's going on for *them*, it becomes harder and harder to access our own feeling states, and to recognize our own needs.

It is possible to learn to work with our sensitive and empathetic nature. With practice and healing, you can fully love another while keeping clear boundaries in place. This means understanding that your needs are separate from your partner's, and that you feeling and expressing your own needs is an important part of keeping balance. Learning that relationships offer a safe place to share your needs as well as meet the needs of another, you will be able to navigate the profound connection that your sensitivity to the feelings of others can foster, and that becomes a conduit not only to a deeper connection with your partner but to a greater, universal love.

This starts with creating an unshakable connection to the world within us. When we are in energetic alignment with ourselves first and foremost, we can shift our focus between our own needs and the needs of our partner. We instinctively know when to put energy into the relationship, or when it's time to retreat back into ourselves to replenish our own reserves. The process of becoming self-full is also about learning what kinds of relationships to lean on that will help you learn trust, feel supported, and heal. Whether you're in a romantic partnership right now, it is important that you find this emotionally available support—be it a therapist, friend, or support group that can provide external support while you do your inner work. Start thinking about who in your world, past or present, may be able to offer this kind of nonjudgmental and unconditional support. Let them know you may be calling on them at times to talk about your experience as you move through this healing process—inner transformation.

IT'S ALL GOOD!

You might be reading this chapter thinking, "This all sounds great, but *my* problem is I keep picking the wrong people." That's an easy mind-set to fall into when you've been burned by a series of messy breakups and car-crash liaisons. But blaming your failed relationships on the inability to choose the right partner is unfair because it implies that you are simply a bad judge of character. The reason you find yourself in these relationships has to do with how you expect to love and be loved. And this goes back to those deeply ingrained patterns from childhood. I've been working with Nina, a thirty-three-year-old, single, gay woman who has a buttoned-up accounting job. She is a conventional person and tends to play it safe in the world. She came to me for help, explaining that she's attracted to "assholes"—women who cheat on her and at times are emotionally abusive by ghosting her when she needs them the most, leaving her in the dust with no explanations. After talking and exploring her feelings, Nina was able to see that she is attracted to rebellious and carefree women because she feels she lacks those qualities within. She did some inner work and discovered that the free spirit in her had been crushed by parents who couldn't tolerate her joy or her urge to explore. As she slowly started to unlock these lost traits, she felt afraid that she would be unlovable if she was even a little more outgoing. Working through these fears, she was able to take more risks. She started taking modern dance classes and shook up her wardrobe to express her more authentic nature, going from buttoned-up oxford shirts to a chic bohemian vibe. She even got a small moon-shaped tattoo. In our sessions, she started speaking up more, and even expressed healthy anger for the first time. All of this led to her challenging her belief system about how she "should" show up in the world. Before long, she found herself having more chemistry with women who were kinder and more stable and began her first long-term relationship in many years.

If, like Nina, you have found yourself in a series of relationships that ended painfully, it doesn't mean that you chose the wrong person yet again. In each relationship, both of you *subconsciously* chose each other, and you did so for good reason. We'll look at this dynamic in depth in the next chapter, but what it is showing you is simply that you have more work to do on yourself. There is more to be learned about who you are, what you need, and what needs healing. When we look at our relationships from the binary perspective of "good" and "bad," "right for me" or "wrong for me," we are not yet looking at our own role in how things played out.

In my relationship with my ex-husband, I felt like the victim of my unhappy marriage, as if everything was happening *to* me and I had no control over the situation whatsoever. But in the years following my divorce, rather than constantly looking for a cure for my broken heart in other relationships, I chose to look within. I faced some loneliness. I rediscovered some friendships and relationships that could help support me as I gained a new sense of myself. You, too, have the opportunity to look more deeply at what unconsciously drives you to attach to people who feed your anxiety, causing you to spiral into panic at the first sign of a problem. If anything, our unhealthy romantic relationships teach us some of our most valuable life lessons. Seen this way, each argument or harrowing breakup can be viewed like a signpost that says "Stop here to heal."

As long as we are willing to look and learn, we can find deep meaning in every interaction. I actually believe that everyone we cross paths with—including our families, friends, teachers, colleagues, and even the people we interact with on social media—has a valuable lesson for us. We just need to be open to receive it. While our interactions with others can fast-track this journey of discovery, we don't even have to be in a relationship to start learning how to become self-full. Sometimes, it is easier to begin this healing journey when we are between intimate relationships since we must do the work ourselves, and the desire must come from within. On the flip side, we also can't compel anyone else to begin this journey with us. We can make a request of our partner, but we can't simply say, "Listen, I'm learning how to heal myself, and you'd better do the same. You've got just as many issues as I do and this won't work unless you fix yours, too." You don't have to be a relationship expert to imagine how that conversation would play out.

Ultimately, you are responsible for yourself, and yourself only. You will be amazed at how much your current and future relationships will improve once you've taken the initiative and done your own inner work. This might seem like a simple fix: Heal your own wounds and your relationship will instantaneously morph into the perfect fairy-tale romance you always dreamed of. But we also have to stay realistic. First of all, no relationship is flawless. No matter how emotionally secure you become, you're going to butt heads with your partner from time to time. A successful relationship is not one without any issues. Instead, the health of your union comes down to how you handle conflicts when they do arise.

Many people discover there is a spiritual dimension to this work. Eventually, you may find yourself aligning energetically with a universal source of love and support so much greater than you even believed possible, a connection you will begin to see reflected in the quality of *all* your relationships. After all, love comes in many forms, from self-love, to romantic love, to divine love, to loving all that is. When you set out to cultivate healthy romantic relationships, make no mistake, you are setting out on a path that can lead to spiritual transformation. It may become a journey that is powerful far beyond finding a partner to create a home with or getting your daily needs met. Entered from a place of inner stability, our relationships can be a pathway to understanding ourselves as spiritual beings, connected to all that is.

CHAPTER 2

The Secret Language of the Little Me Pact

While a marriage contract could be seen as the icing on the cake when it comes to making a romantic commitment to another person, the truth is we enter into an *emotional pact* with each and every person with whom we develop an intimate bond. As people become closer to each other, they gradually feel safe enough to reveal more of their inner worlds, including parts of themselves they're afraid their partners may not like. Perhaps one person begins to show that he or she gets frustrated about certain things. Or the other person acknowledges that watching sports on TV is something he or she finds important. At this time of increased vulnerability, the ways each of them learned to love and be loved as children begin to stir within them. The question "Will you still love me if . . ." begins to play in the back of their hearts. And the emotional pacts they made the last time they felt this vulnerable, in early childhood, become an important part of the relationship.

If you think about it, every interaction we perform throughout our day involves some kind of exchange. Whether it's paying for groceries in the store, showing up for work in exchange for a salary, or trading gossip with our friends, every investment of our time, energy, or cold, hard cash is made with the expectation that we will receive something in return. This doesn't make us calculated, manipulative, or greedy. It's just the way the world works. The same way the trees breathe in carbon dioxide and pump fresh oxygen back out into the atmosphere, giving and receiving is a part of life. Seen this way, it makes sense that this dynamic also forms the basis of our romantic relationships.

While a mutual exchange of understanding, support, and unconditional love is what we all want when we enter into a "contract" with a potential life partner, our capacity to experience this is profoundly impacted by our childhood experiences and the attachment style we have developed as a result. Part of our inherent wisdom is that we are able to adapt to the way in which our primary caregivers tended to our basic needs (or not). Since connection is a biological imperative, we devote all of our energy to staying as attached to our parents as we can. This is the origin of the emotional pact we bring into our intimate relationships. Let's look more closely at how these get established.

We are so open and vulnerable in our earliest days, and so dependent on the support of our caregivers. By the time we're one year old, we have already developed patterns of interaction with our parents based on how they are able to be with us. If our parents can sense our needs, if they can be warmly curious about who we are as little beings, welcoming every part of us, if they are able to respond to us when we reach out, we are on the way to being securely attached. This ingrains the expectation that we will be met, valued, and supported in relationship with others. Clearly, we are lovable. Rather than being based on a thought or belief, this *knowing* is generated by the feelings in our bodies in relationships. It might include warmth in the chest, a relaxed belly, a general sense of openness, and easy laughter. It will also include tears that are met with concern, validation, and help. All of this brings our ANS into the ventral state over and over, weaving together the neural circuitry of emotional regulation. What a gift!

But some parents are too wounded to provide that kind of care. If one or both of our parents are anxious, they may be able to be with us sometimes, but they will get pulled away by their own inner upset unexpectedly and frequently. This unpredictability leaves us not knowing when they will next disconnect from us, making us frightened and hypervigilant. When we are young, we soon learn which of our behaviors lead to our parents' disappearances and begin to suppress those parts. With no thought involved at all, we can begin to stop ourselves from healthy expressions of joy or sadness or anger in the effort to keep our parents with us. Meanwhile, our ANS is spending way too much time in sympathetic arousal, leaving us almost continually afraid of loss and abandonment. We bring this legacy into our adult relationships, tucked away in our subconscious, until it becomes activated with the prospect of intimacy.

Now, *everything we never learned* about how to connect rises to the surface.

Kids whose parents are wrapped up in their careers, and who value good behavior and success above all else, also learn early on that relationships aren't important compared to being able to do well in the world. Left on our own, we will often play quietly, without joy, and when our parents return, we show little interest in connecting with them. While these parents are often interested in helping us develop skills, they are at a loss when we are sad or scared. It's as though half of us, the intellectual part, is supported, while the other half, the emotional, relational part, is neglected. We have gotten so used to constant pressure and the threat of shame that it seems normal to us, but researchers tell us that this kind of emotional abandonment leads to almost constant sympathetic arousal. When we come into relationships as adults, we find ourselves lost and bewildered in the face of intimacy. We may be quite competent in the world, yet struggle to understand why this isn't enough to make our partner happy. When our partner's neediness increases, we get freaked out and turn to work as the only source of connection we know.

Of course, each of us is unique, and each of our early experiences of connection will be different. But as you read this, you may recognize invisible tendencies that developed very young as you sought to connect with your caregivers. Given that connection is the most fundamental need we have, we will literally twist ourselves into whatever pretzel shape is required to feel like we belong.

GETTING TO KNOW LITTLE ME

Little Me is what we keep referring to as the younger part of you, which you may have recognized in the above descriptions. As we are developing, any time our body feels something, these feelings get sent to our brain, where we turn them into "stories" to help us make sense of what we're experiencing. For example, if we're feeling sad or scared because of how someone else is showing up, we might feel like there is something wrong with us. Little Me (who still exists as part of you today) has stored these experiences, feelings, and stories as memories in the subconscious part of the brain. Both the core wounds and the core support we received as kids live here, and these embodied memories go on to play a powerful role in our behaviors as adults—especially when it comes to relationships.

You'll be getting to know your Little Me a lot better in the coming chapters, as Little Me plays a key role when it comes to being anxiously attached. For now, consider this: Given that Little Me has the power to influence our actions and our choices in ways that are often completely hidden to us, is it any wonder that we find ourselves making the same "mistakes" in love, time and again? What our adult self may *consciously* see as bad decisions and red flags are often very familiar to the part of our brain that believes, deep down, that *this is what love feels like*. Let's take a look at how this works.

Picture two fourth-graders meeting on the playground at school. One of the children, Ben, has a mother who shows very little emotion and who is hyper-focused on her career. Despite being a top-level accountant at a rather stressful job, she is able to show up for Ben in many ways—including helping him with his homework and praising him when he has done something well. She attends his football games and often expresses how proud she is of him. But she struggles knowing how to show up for Ben emotionally, such as when he expresses sadness or anger. In fact, she often doesn't notice his emotional states. Any time he's upset, she helps him figure out how to "fix the problem" rather than simply listening and validating how he is feeling. None of this makes her a "bad" mom—she is simply showing Ben love in the same ways *she* received love as a child. She also grew up with parents who struggled with emotional connection and focused more on praising her accomplishments. Because young children shape themselves around their parents' needs and values, Ben believes that to receive love he must always "do well" and so, over time, he places more and more emphasis on doing things that he feels proud of, while simultaneously minimizing awareness of his emotional states since it hurts when they go unnoticed. At school, his independent attitude means he comes across externally as self-assured, and his classmate Hunter finds herself very drawn to his confidence.

Meanwhile, in Hunter's home, things are quite different. Her mother is often preoccupied with her own anxiety and doesn't seem to have much time for her daughter. The demands of running the home and having a career she doesn't like make it hard for her mom to notice what Hunter needs. Sometimes, her mother calms down enough to read a story and cuddle Hunter, but mostly she just seems frazzled and distracted. As a result, Hunter has experienced that love comes and goes in unpredictable ways, which scares her. She has become hypervigilant to her mother's emotional needs, so she can do the little things that seem to help her mother be more available—being quiet, keeping her room clean, not asking for much. The small doses of affection she does receive feel so good that Hunter has learned to put her own needs second, going out of her way to please her mother. She feels she must work hard to earn her mother's love. When this doesn't work, however, her feelings of being ignored often overflow, causing her to cling to her mom in desperation. Back at school, Ben is drawn to Hunter's attentiveness, her kindness, and her open nature.

Over time, Hunter and Ben become friends—and in doing so, make an unspoken *Little Me Pact* based on the core beliefs that have already been imprinted in them about what it means to give and receive love. Ben will impress Hunter with his independence, making her feel "special and seen" when he chooses to spend time with her. In return, Hunter will shower him with attention no matter what, and he will feel "special and seen" by her. It's as if they each instinctively know what the other needs to feel loved and appreciated. And while the friendship is mutually beneficial at first, after a while being around each other feels unnatural and strained. While Hunter is craving more attention, Ben begins to feel confused and no longer competent. Hunter begins to resent having to work so hard at maintaining their connection, and when she speaks up by getting emotional, Ben feels overwhelmed by her expression of feelings and begins to retreat. Feeling rejected, Hunter gets even more angry at him. Eventually they have a fight—and the friendship is over.

Are these children to blame for how things played out? Were

they being naïve when they became friends or intentionally setting themselves up for a falling-out? Of course not. When it comes to forming attachments with others, they don't know any better. All they want is to feel acknowledged, accepted, and loved for who they are, and they are simply behaving in the ways they have learned will help them receive the love and attention they need.

WHERE OUR CORE WOUNDS COME FROM

Hunter and Ben's story illustrates how core attachment wounds are created in childhood and how these wounds go on to influence the texture of our relationships. Ben's home life lacked acknowledgment of emotions, so he has developed an avoidant attachment style in order to stay connected with his unemotional parents. Having received inconsistent attention from her mother, Hunter has become anxiously attached as she struggles to get the little bits of attention her mother is able to offer if conditions are just right. As such, their friendship follows a pattern that will become all too familiar to them as they navigate their adult relationships, as each of their intimate connections will be based on the same Little Me Pact.

Why? When left unexamined, core wounds that are formed in childhood and the embodied relational patterns attached to them will continue to control our behaviors from behind the scenes of our adult lives. When there are unhealed wounds, this part of us never grows up. While we may think we are entering into our romantic relationships as two fully formed adults, our wounded Little Me is in fact often doing the only thing they know how to do.

These core wounds take root in early childhood as a result of having one or more of our basic emotional needs unmet. Some parents miss the mark a little bit, others miss it most of the time. We need safety, attention, reflection, love, and leisurely connection. As we saw in the last chapter, during infancy and early childhood, we rely on our primary caregivers to meet these needs. When for whatever reason this does not happen, we slip into a state of emotional disarray. This likely happens even in a fully functioning home environment. Our parents are only human, and the sheer pace of modern life, coupled with a lack of support from the wider family group, means they can't be expected to meet one hundred percent of our needs at any given time of the day. However, when they miss us and are able to acknowledge it as well as offer times of unconditional love and joy in our presence, it is enough to develop secure attachment. If one or more of our needs remains consistently unmet and our parents aren't able to notice or repair the injury, we develop a core wound around this need. Ben needed it to be safe for him to have emotions, and Hunter needed a mother consistent enough to provide security. Their resulting adaptations got them as much care as their parents could offer but fell far short of what they actually needed. So both are moving toward adulthood with wounds firmly entrenched.

This is a good place to take a break for some reflection. As you read this, are you beginning to sense ways in which your parents met your need for safety, attention, reflection, love, and leisurely connection? And ways in which they couldn't? Even with the best intentions, our parents have their wounds as well, and this often makes it hard for them to give us what they didn't get. Pausing here for a bit and just listening to what is in your heart about this can begin our journey down this road together.

Our attachment experiences with our parents have a lot to do with how our brains develop. How does this work? The amygdala is one important part of the brain that is involved in our emotional response to threatening situations. In order for it to perform this function, it is imprinted with memories of how we responded to fearful events in childhood, creating a blueprint for how we respond to similar situations in the future. This is one way our brains work to keep us safe. If my parents need me to sit up perfectly straight at the dinner table in order to accept me, my brain will warn me not to slump, even when I'm the CEO of my own company. The message comes so quickly that we react *without thinking* in the face of what we perceive to be immediate threats to our safety. Clearly, there's no danger in me slumping, but my brain isn't living in the now. Instead, the old message about slumping is fully alive in this moment. This is a small, inconsequential example, but when this "threat" looks less like whether to follow the impulse to slump and more like a romantic partner who appears cold and distant, the stakes are much higher.

Specific to how Hunter and Ben interact, the core wound of abandonment gets activated in the anxious one. For people who are attached in this way, the fear of being abandoned stems from a lack of consistent attention to their needs, resulting in an attachment system that has to be constantly on guard, with an ANS in sympathetic arousal. This means that their amygdalae become hypersensitive to signs of abandonment. Their natural adaptive response is to focus on the other person's needs and if that doesn't work, to cling in desperation in an attempt to have the other person soothe their ANS. For people with an avoidant attachment style, there has been a core wounding related to emotional neglect. In their childhoods, their emotions went unnoticed, so their brains built a wall between the part that feels that need and is in terrible pain because it is unmet and the part that can focus on performing. When they feel the threat of intimacy, which would expose them to the enormous pain of not having their emotions acknowledged, their system shuts down and focuses on the tasks at hand. It all happens automatically for both people, attempting to protect them from the intolerable pain of their core wounds.

In order to become fully functional in your interpersonal relationships, it is vital to take time to acknowledge and to sit with this wounded Little Me. I will be accompanying you as you learn how to be present for these harder experiences you had as a child. I will guide you on how to listen to the little child inside, so you can give them the attention and care they didn't receive when they were young. This is the work of becoming self-full, and I will be supporting you through the exact process of how to do this in part two of this book. But first, we must identify the core wounds we are carrying. This is step one in rewriting the adapted but painful Little Me Pacts that are the foundation of our relationship struggles.

♥♥

WHERE DOES IT HURT?

To recap, we develop a core wound when one of our basic needs remains consistently unmet. Over time, this leads to the formation of the protective patterns that go on to influence our behavior and the way we relate to others. Usually developed during childhood, these wounds become so calcified over time, and the relational patterns attached to them so deeply ingrained, that we carry them with us wherever we go so that they become the lens through which we see the world, coloring our perception of every interaction. Over time, we become so accustomed to living with our core wounds, and simultaneously so attached to the beliefs they have instilled in us, that they seem like they are simply who we are. We become this adapted version of ourselves.

Let's take a close look at my client Carrie, who is doing her best to find love, but her wounds keep her from forming deeper intimacy. When Carrie was evaluating why none of her relationships seemed to work, she found she consistently felt disappointed after the courting phase, when men became less interested in her looks and wanted a deeper connection. As the kind of attention they paid her changed, she began to feel anxious, then lost and alone. From the time she was quite small, her parents showered her with attention at times, but it was always on the theme of how beautiful she was. The rest of the time, they dismissed her and returned their focus to their busy careers. She began to feel that the only valuable thing about her was her beauty, so any time she felt confused, sad, or scared, she simply pushed those parts of herself away as unworthy of care. This pattern generated the thoughts: "All that matters is how I look" and "There's nothing else worthwhile in me."

Of course, this was not the case, but since it was the only aspect reflected by her parents as being of value, she had no way to develop other parts of herself. She felt so much pain when her mother would say, "Stop crying. No one likes red eyes," or her father would assure her, "You don't have to worry about how you do in school because your beauty will open all the doors." One of the most wounding parts of Carrie's experience was that she was never allowed to explore her own interests. When Carrie told her parents that she would love to take an art class or two, they immediately shut her down: "What's the point? Art won't get you anywhere in life, and you already have too much on your plate." When she told her mom she was upset about something, her mother would say, "I understand that hurts, but hey, at least you're beautiful." At no point, did Carrie feel like her own authentic voice was heard.

With all of her attention going toward maintaining this outer façade, not only did she not have a chance to develop her considerable artistic ability, she also failed to learn that feelings like sadness and anger are also important parts of her. Instead, she developed a deep core wound of shame. Over time, her feelings of worthlessness developed into the adult belief that she must be loved first and foremost for her beauty, or she would begin to feel the deep abandonment she experienced when her parents ignored her rich emotional life. It was as if there was a constant voice in her head that said, "Whatever you do, don't let them take their eyes off you!"

But wait, can't she just keep searching until she finds a partner who will stay focused on her physical appearance? Sadly, it's not that simple. Since this core wound has become part of Carrie, she brings it with her to every relationship, transmitting the message to her partners: "You must continue to see me as most beautiful and never want more from me." Meanwhile, deep inside, her strongest conviction is "While I know I am beautiful, I don't have anything more to offer." If she unconsciously attracts a partner who is only interested in her appearance, she suffers the same pain as she did with her parents. If she attracts someone who genuinely wants to know her more deeply, she feels panic when this person no longer focuses on her beauty. This core wound literally left her with nowhere to turn.

If this is all going on behind the scenes without us even realizing, how are we supposed to interrupt the pattern? The first thing is to remember that it's not our partner's job to fix us, and neither is it on us to find somebody who will miraculously understand us and know how to heal our wounds. Our focus is to identify our wound, to look at where it came from, and to connect to and heal the pain and fear that keep the thoughts and behaviors in place. Until we are able to do this, the patterns getting repeated in our relationships will continue to follow a very similar script.

As time passes, a wound like Carrie's may scab over. However, it will repeatedly be reopened in every intimate relationship, and soon she will simply grow accustomed to the pain. Even more tragic is that we are often drawn, as if by an energetic magnet, to reexperience these core wounds *because a deep part of us believes them to be true.*

Examples of common beliefs that form around our most frequent relational experiences during our young lives include:

- I am going to be abandoned.
- I am unlovable.
- I will be rejected if I show my true self.
- I am going to be humiliated or embarrassed.
- I cannot trust others.
- I am not good enough.
- I have to work hard to earn love.
- I need people, but I can't rely on them.
- It's my job to keep other people happy.
- Other people are always taking from me.
- The world is an unsafe place.
- Bad things always happen to me.
- People only love me when I do well.

STEPS TO RECOGNIZE YOUR CORE WOUNDS

To begin to get familiar with your own core wounds, let's continue with Carrie's story as you work through these steps.

Step One: Who do you attract?

When taking a look at her personal relationship history, Carrie found that she always ends up with partners with these characteristics: They are infatuated with her, career-oriented, and emotionally present when they are in pursuit of her but drop her when they feel her committing to them. On a deeper level, her partners tend to be so devoted to success that she often feels lonely and abandoned when they focus back on their work lives. Ask yourself:

- What qualities do your romantic partners tend to have in common?
- What is the common theme of how they treat you in relationships?

Step Two: How do you relate?

Carrie is attracted to crisp, good-looking businessmen who have attained a high level of success. They are attracted to her because she seems sexy and self-confident. However, these men are able to show up for her in the beginning but then get so wrapped up in their careers that their emotional lives come second. They are never available for important conversations and don't know how to talk about their feelings. As a result, Carrie begins to feel emotionally needy around them, often holding on to their attention by dressing sexily but later feeling a sense of abandonment because the relationship lacks a deeper connection. Ask yourself:

- Where are the gaps in your communication with your partners?
- What do you not feel free to express?
- What goes unheard when you do express it?

- What are the negative feelings you repeatedly experience in your relationships?

Step Three: Travel back in time.

Carrie's mother was very beautiful and valued her appearance, and her father was an accomplished lawyer who focused almost exclusively on his work. She basically got praise and love for her looks, and no one spent time really helping her learn more about her whole self. She even remembers a time when they told her, "Don't worry, honey, you're so beautiful you will never have a problem finding a boyfriend." As a result, she often felt torn between admiration for them and sadness that she felt empty inside. This pointed to a core abandonment wound that she could see had continued to play out in her relationships, leading to the belief that *People only value me for my appearance and end up leaving me.* Ask yourself:

- What was lacking in the caregiving you received as a young person?
- Can you remember a specific incident when you experienced this?
- What do you feel in your body when you touch into this experience?
- What belief or beliefs about how you receive love may have stemmed from this?
- How do your relationships today reflect what you experienced in childhood?

Step Four: Chart your pattern.

So that you can get really clear on how your core childhood wounds continue to play out in your intimate relationships, create a chart to track them. First, write down any core wounds you have identified, along with any beliefs connected to them. Next, describe how you first experienced each of them in childhood. Finally, record the ways they have been reactivated in your adult relationships. Here's an example from Carrie's chart.

My Core Wound	I will always get left.
An Example of This in My Childhood	Neither of my parents helped me understand other aspects of myself.
Belief That I Learned About Myself	My needs are not important, and my role is to look the part.
How This Continues to Play Out Today	I tend to attract lots of men but none of them want to get to know me.
Bodily Sensations and Emotional Feelings That Come Up	Sadness, pain in my heart, tightness in my belly, depression

By charting her patterns, Carrie also realized that any time her core wound is activated she stifles the part of herself that feels abandoned and goes on with her day-to-day life. After all, her partners (like her parents) have always taken care of her physical needs for shelter and food, so she feels she should be grateful, even as the lack of unconditional acceptance leaves her feeling empty inside. In order to learn from past relationships, take some time to think about how you respond when a core wound gets touched or activated. For example, do you tend to run and hide, or react with an emotion like anger or sadness? Do you shut down emotionally, or spiral down a rabbit hole of negative self-talk?

Carrie's abandonment wound is merely an example. Maybe your parents had money troubles and borrowed money from your summer job to help pay the bills. This could result in a pattern whereby you attract partners who are jobless, broke, and reliant upon you for security, reinforcing the belief that you must provide financial security for somebody to love you. Maybe you always push people away three months into a relationship because your core wound says no one is trustworthy. Or perhaps you cling desperately to your relationships long after it becomes clear they aren't working since your core wound is a terror of being alone. Whatever you recognize as your core wounds and the painful patterns attached to them, we can begin the process of healing them. Even awareness can help in the meantime, since you will be more likely to sense when it is time to slow down and focus on healing rather than push ahead in a new relationship. If you remain unaware of them, you could find yourself in a similar situation to Susan and Dan.

SUSAN AND DAN

To the outside world, Susan and Dan seem relatively happy together. But behind closed doors they have been grappling with some issues. Although they like to eat out, Susan also makes dinner regularly. When she does, she asks Dan to help her clean up the kitchen and load the dishwasher. Most of the time, Dan remembers and willingly helps her clean up when the meal is over. But sometimes her request slips his mind, usually when he is exhausted after a long day at work and just wants to veg out in front of the television.

When this happens, Susan feels upset and unappreciated. But she is afraid to voice her frustration because her wounded Little Me fears that upsetting Dan will lead to him leaving her. Her core abandonment wound means that she believes on a deep, subconscious level that she will only receive his love if she can keep Dan happy—a common belief in those who are anxiously attached. And so instead of speaking up and letting Dan know it bothers her when he forgets to clean the kitchen, she minimizes her need for help and recognition and becomes even more attentive to Dan's needs to compensate.

Until one random Sunday evening, when Susan prepared a beautiful dinner. She spent all afternoon in the kitchen to prep, cook, and bake. Dan had been looking forward to watching a sporting event all day, so after dinner he quickly retreated to the den and turned on the game. Susan exploded. She could not contain her frustration any longer. All the anger that had been building up inside came pouring out: She insulted Dan and called him names, smashed some dishes and the ensuing fight led to a major rupture in the relationship.

Dan had no idea how upset his lack of involvement in the cleanup process made Susan feel. He was completely oblivious, not because he was a bad partner, but because Susan never expressed her agitation. Sure, he knew she appreciated his help. But Susan had been stifling her needs and emotional authenticity out of fear of losing him. She avoided conflict to the point where it had nowhere to go, and the resentments built up until Susan's wounded Little Me had no option but to blow up. Unconsciously, she had created a scenario in which her fear of Dan leaving her was one step closer to coming true.

A FATAL ATTRACTION

Now let's take a look at how Little Me Pacts play out in the world of adult dating. Two people meet on a popular dating app. The connection is instant. Conversation flows readily and feels incredibly natural. They begin texting more and more, and before long they are spending a lot of time together. First, they meet for coffee. Then drinks. Soon they are meeting up three to four times a week.

From an outside perspective, the progression of the relationship seems normal and healthy. Isn't this kind of connection what everybody's looking for? What isn't so obvious is that each of them have a Little Me who is also part of the relationship from the beginning. If these little ones have received the nurturance they needed to become securely attached, we can imagine that this relationship will unfold fairly easily. However, if one or both of them are carrying significant core wounds, it is likely that below conscious awareness they also saw something in each other that felt familiar from the past. It is amazing how sensitive our systems are to what is going on inside the other person. I once had a client who said that if I lined up twenty men, she would immediately go toward the one who was a serial cheater without knowing anything about him. We are all coming into relationships with our own unconscious expectations, which will play out as our connection evolves.

Expectations can vary significantly. Perhaps it is to re-create and reenact old childhood wounds so that we can attempt to fix ourselves at last. Perhaps it is to keep us sheltered and safe from our biggest fears, such as the fear of being abandoned or of being wholly responsible for another person's well-being. Or perhaps—as in the kind of healthy relationship described in chapter 1—it is to learn more about ourselves and to grow spiritually.

While it's often impossible to identify at the beginning of a relationship, recognizing the subconscious pact between your Little Me and your partner's once you hit the first snag will help you discover where there is some deeper work to do. For example, when Julie began getting more in touch with her Little Me, she realized that the relationship with her new partner, Steve, was activating old wounds. Julie was the youngest of four siblings, so her emotional needs were not always met during childhood. She didn't receive the attention she needed because her parents were spread very thin. On the other hand, when she met Steve, she found him to be attentive and extremely available. Her needs were met by him immediately, and for a while, Julie's Little Me felt safe and loved. But over time, Steve had become more and more controlling. It became clear that he was only willing to show up emotionally if he could take charge. This led to Julie's authentic needs and sense of self being sidelined. Instead of being loved and supported, now she felt trapped. Her work was to see where needing his attention took over from her ability to tend to her own inner world, leading to self-abandonment.

Spend some time with your current and past relationships. Can you begin to sense the nature of the Little Me Pacts you have unwittingly made with your different partners? "If you stay with him, you'll never be alone," one Little Me might have promised. "I'll let you make all the decisions if you will stay with me," another might have said.

Going back to the idea that all our interpersonal relationships are built on a foundation of mutual reciprocity, it makes sense that we want to partner up with somebody who "gets us" and seems to know what we need. Problems arise when this agreement requires a disavowal of either partner's whole, authentic self. In this scenario, it is inevitable that both of you will begin to form resentments toward each other. The result? Frustration, animosity, and blame, and yet another "failed" relationship. Furthermore, once a pact of this nature has been made, it becomes so much harder to identify and heal the core wounds it has been founded on. It is as if you have been blinded by love.

THE ENERGETIC DANCE OF RELATIONSHIPS

Let's look at this from a little different angle. Remember how I said that our core wounds act like an *energetic magnet*? Let's first take a look at how energy actually works. Quantum theory shows us that everything in the universe is made of energy, including our thoughts and feelings, which have their own electromagnetic charge. This means that our thoughts alone (both our conscious thoughts and our subconscious core patterns) have the power to "magnetically attract" situations that fit their energetic imprint. This explains why we feel mysteriously drawn to some people more than others. Simply put, their beliefs about themselves and the world make them an energetic match for us.

This also shows how the energy of any patterns created by our core wounds can find us signing the same pain-inducing Little Me Pacts in our relationships time and time again. For example, if Hunter subconsciously believes "I must work hard to earn love," then she will be projecting the energy of this belief into her world, thus attracting situations and relationships that prove this to be true. Unconsciously, she is literally re-creating this reality with her inner expectations.

Because our Little Me holds on to past wounds until they can be healed (through the process of becoming self-full), the energy—or emotional charge—of these wounds remains trapped within us. As energetic beings, we rely on a free-flowing source of energy to function properly in the world. Without any way for the *trapped* energy of our core wounds to be released, it builds over time, resulting in emotional outbursts (as we saw in Susan's story) or else manifesting in emotional issues such as anxiety, depression, addiction, and self-harm. When issues such as these show up, it is a sign that our wounded Little Me does not feel safe—and is looking for ways to self-soothe—including new intimate relationships that appear to offer exactly the balm (a fresh supply of energy) that we have been searching for (manifesting as an insatiable "hunger" for attachment). But when we enter into a Little Me Pact with another person from this place, our own emotional energy is not flowing freely or being replenished.

As a result of this stagnant energy, we also begin to lack creativity and spontaneity, and can feel deflated, uneasy, and unfulfilled. We struggle to access our higher self or to find any kind of spiritual connection or meaning in the world. We become disconnected from our intuition and our innate sense of knowing when something is right or wrong for us, making it impossible to make decisions that are in our best interest. Even when we think we are doing something beneficial for ourselves, we may actually be causing more harm. Essentially, we are living in survival mode, and as a result life feels empty of authentic, lasting joy and fulfillment.

Entering into a partnership with the energy of our core wounds taking the lead means that rather than choosing a mate who will help us to open up and grow, we are simply using the relationship as another quick fix. At first, we may feel distracted or temporarily soothed by the new energy that this new person brings into our life. Maybe, as the relationship inevitably sours, we get some relief from being able to blame our pain on them. But the longer we avoid facing the root cause of this trapped energy and actively working to release it, the longer we will remain stuck in it.

Now let's compare this with the experience of creating an intimate bond from an emotionally healthy place. When we become conscious of our core wounds, we can recognize what areas of our lives require attention and then heal these wounds with the support of caring others. The Little Me Pact we make with a partner from this place is based on a *mutual exchange of free-flowing energy*. This is what it means to be self-full. For example, Rachel begins to feel isolated from her peers. Her job leaves her too tired to get out much, so while she has a partner, there is no real sense of community in her life. In a self-full state, Rachel is able to hold space for her own feelings of loneliness and separation. She is aware that she often felt this way in her childhood and notices that these feelings are as old as she is. She shares these feelings with her best friend, who is really good at listening without fixing. This keeps her from reacting by running to her partner to fix her, or blaming her partner for her feelings of loneliness. As her Little Me feels met and cared for, Rachel begins to attend to her need for community. She may purchase a monthly membership to a local yoga studio or join a nonfiction book club that discusses topics she is passionate about. Recognizing her own unmet need for community, she takes positive steps to create this for herself.

But without this awareness and movement toward healing, her own energy flow becomes blocked or inaccessible to her, and Rachel's automatic reaction may be to immerse herself more deeply in her romantic relationship. She chooses to spend even more time with her partner, doting on him in the hope that he will give her what she needs in return. She may grow frustrated and resentful when he wants to spend time with friends or go to the gym on his own. By now, Rachel has grown dependent upon her partner to fulfill all of her needs—even those he is simply not qualified to meet. As a result, she becomes depressed and their relationship becomes strained.

The second version of Rachel's story shows a classic example of somebody slipping into *codependency*, the term used to describe relationships in which one or both partners are focusing on the other's needs in order to protect themselves from feeling their own pain and fear. Yes, we are interdependent beings and we all need connection with others, but when this connection is based on fear or when our partner becomes our sole source of emotional and energetic nourishment and support, codependency sets in. As we will discover in the next chapter, in this scenario we become so attuned and empathetic to our partner's needs that we neglect our own, often out of fear that asking to have our needs met will lead to rejection or abandonment. As a result, we unconsciously attract others who "need" us, mistaking this for them "loving" us. Responding from fear blocks the flow of energy and overwhelms our intuition.

To help you picture the way energy works, let's imagine a solid line of energy connecting your head to your heart. Interestingly, this is also the neural pathway that activates when we are in the ventral state and open to safe connection. This line of energy begins above our head, connecting us to the universal energy flow, runs through our brain, and to our heart. When we are centered and in alignment, energy flows easily between these three centers, allowing them to connect and exchange information with one another. When this system is running smoothly, we are able to replenish our own energetic resources by connecting to the inner resources we have developed in our healing. We become our own self-renewing source of free-flowing energy. We become more able to make choices that are in alignment with the person we are today, rather than acting on the subconscious patterns that have been put in place to appease and soothe our wounded Little Me. What's more, we are able to bring free-flowing new energy into our relationships, helping both us and our partner to grow.

Now let's say that one of these energy centers has become blocked as a result of an unexamined core wound. Maybe the heart has closed out of fear of abandonment (like Susan), so that we have disconnected from our own feelings in order to make someone else happy. Or we knowingly lie to our partner to avoid his or her criticism, creating a tight knot of paranoia in our belly and brain. Perhaps we ignore the calling of our soul for fear of being alone, deaf to our intuition and making life choices that are not for our highest good. In each of these examples, a core wound is being activated, our energy flow has become blocked, and we may begin to rely solely on our partner to regulate our energy system.

When we continually only look to an external force to stabilize and give us energy, we lose our center and the relationship will become lopsided. This means that if we enter a relationship placing *all* our safety in our romantic partner without developing the ability to regulate and charge our own energy system, our relationship will run out of steam. If our only sense of safety comes from the relationship and suddenly the relationship struggles, we're likely to immobilize our energy system and frantically do whatever it takes to gain access to the other person's. Now we start giving all this energy away because we're scared and this leads us to feeling completely depleted. Over time—and sometimes overnight—we will come to rely only on the other person to keep us safe. Instead of healthy interdependence, we have slipped into codependence. This journey probably feels familiar to many who are anxiously attached. In the following chapter, we'll spend time with the dance that develops between anxious and avoidant people, seeking to deepen compassion and understanding in preparation for entering our own healing work.

CHAPTER 3

The Anxious-Avoidant
Dance and More

A s we discussed in chapter 1, secure attachments are formed
from our ability to co-regulate with our primary caregivers;
often this starts with a maternal figure. If she is attuned to
our needs, this capacity for co-regulation develops naturally in us.
In the early days after birth, when we are just meeting each other,
babies don't have the advantage of being able to say, "Mom, I need
you to pick me up," or "Mom, I'm hungry." Instead, co-regulation
happens in a dance of joyful facial expressions, response to our cries,
and the tone of voice that tells us she is attuned to us. All of this is
fueled by the interplay of unseen chemical interactions. Mom won't
always get it right the first time, but if she is attending to us, she will
keep trying until we are able to settle together—into play or rest.
Each time this happens, our very young brains are being wired for

this dance of connection: a dance that plays out in our romantic relationships as adults.

In a healthy and mutually supportive relationship, this ability to attend to each other and offer cues of safety plays a role in helping each partner decipher how best to respond to what their lover needs. But when two people come together who did not learn how to co-regulate in childhood—the underlying issue for those with either an anxious or an avoidant attachment style—they literally have no capacity to truly see and be with each other, and the results can be either explosive or quietly miserable. This is especially true when these two polar opposites attract. Each looks to the other for what they missed in childhood and neither of them is able to provide it.

Ultimately, we all have the same need for unconditional love, support, and understanding. While those who are anxiously attached express this in a desire for constant connection and reassurance, avoidant people feel safest when they are allowed plenty of space and independence. Remember the theory behind the Little Me Pact? These differing relational blueprints developed as survival strategies in response to inconsistent or emotionally neglectful caregiving in early childhood and are triggered anytime we encounter a similar pattern in our adult relationships. Ultimately, we're attracted to behaviors that confirm our subconscious belief that *this is what love feels like*. We confuse what feels *familiar* with what feels *right*, even as we become more and more destabilized by our partner's behavior, causing anxious people to cling even harder, and avoidant people to detach emotionally and shut down.

When anxious meets avoidant, it's like two opposite ends of a magnet coming together. Stable, secure, intuitive connection is much harder to establish because neither partner feels safe and so both move into sympathetic activation, making connection and co-regulation impossible. Beyond a simple case of crossed wires, they are actually not able to attune to each other's needs. Each person is doing relationship the only way they know how, so the behaviors and the feelings they stir up consistently appear to prove the other's deepest fears to be right. For people who are anxiously attached, partners who constantly pull away prove that they are inherently unlovable and will always be abandoned. Two forces begin to pull at this person: "I have to make them stay!" and "I cannot trust them. They will surely leave me." This leads to behaviors that are almost certain to prove the second statement to be true, so clinging behaviors become more and more desperate.

Avoidant people have a different struggle inside. Either they learned that the only parts of them that were valued were those that focused on work and success, proper behavior, and not showing much emotion; or their families were so chaotic that their only refuge was to pull away. In either case, their parents had little capacity to attune to their needs, and relationships weren't considered important. In other words, these parents didn't have the capacity to offer co-regulation, so the circuitry for secure connection never got built. But since connection is a biological imperative, avoidant people who adapted by putting away all need for emotional support also have an enormous well of pain inside where the legitimate needs for comfort and care weren't met. When anxiously attached people begin to pull on them, they are in a fight for their lives because the emotional attention threatens to open that well of pain. Usually completely out of awareness, their inner world is screaming this warning: "If you let this person in, you'll die of the pain inside you." At a more conscious level, the thought often is "This person is unstable and not behaving properly." Following the family pattern, they simply withdraw.

Given that both partners subconsciously play an equal role in this dance, we're going to take a closer look at the core wounds that awaken and then become the behaviors that stoke the drama in anxious-avoidant relationships. Remember, these are simply examples of both partners doing what they can to protect themselves and that the intention is (usually) not to cause harm. These actions and behaviors are activated by a felt lack of safety. They all come from a place of survival and can be seen through a lens of compassion.

For us anxious people, what we could call our *attachment alarm* is set off whenever something external or internal signals that we may soon be abandoned. Our Little Me's inner world has been touched and we become obsessed with reestablishing closeness with our partner. Internal worries about being left combine with external cues of detachment to move us out of a calm state and into the fight-or-flight response of the sympathetic nervous system. Because the old pattern is firing strongly, our bodies are reexperiencing the struggle to regain connection with our parents and the pain that arose when we couldn't. In that moment, the past becomes the present, making it impossible to have clarity about what is happening right now.

The terror surging through our system sometimes causes us to "flee" and not seek reconnection at all, but most often it urges us to "turn up the volume" energetically to regain connection. We become like an octopus, expanding our energy by reaching out in all directions as we engage in a series of what are called *activating strategies*. Driven by fear and desire, these behaviors will continue until we get a response that reassures us the relationship is intact. Even though our partners have now responded, Little Me's core wounds are not healed by this temporary return, so inwardly we remain on guard for the next sign of possible abandonment. It is very hard for Little Me to find the firm ground of safety very often.

Because of this ongoing fear, certain activating strategies are present most of the time. We may do something as innocuous as constantly talking about someone because this keeps the idea of them in mind (and therefore close, within reach) at all times. No partner will be constantly physically available to us, but it feels as though that's what we need because of the painful absences of childhood that have been reawakened in this intimate relationship.

Another behavior that might sound familiar is if we are unable to get ahold of our partner for an extended period of time, and no reason was previously given for why this might be, we might require our partner to get back in touch as soon as they are able *and* to provide an explanation for the absence in order to calm our attachment system down. Partners who understand this will be able to take little steps to create the reassurance we need and help us feel more secure: a text to let us know they'll be late and why, or information about their upcoming schedule. But when this is not the case, the activating strategies may escalate and become more impulsive as our Little Me grows more certain of abandonment and more desperate in their attempts to secure our partner's attention.

This is often the stage that follows the constant, selfless giving that is the first layer of protective behavior. As long as that keeps our partner close, we remain relatively calm on the outside, although we are still on edge internally. When we feel them slipping away—sometimes because of just doing life, sometimes because of backing away—then we move to this second layer of protective behaviors. We are always on guard for any sign that we could possibly interpret as potential abandonment because the pain of our early losses is like a tension spring just waiting to be released. Then we are flung into the outer space of runaway sympathetic activation where these other behaviors seek to control our inner panic and certainty that we are surely losing them this time.

Constant attempts to make contact. Sending many texts (especially if our partner doesn't answer right away), excessive calling, or hanging around places the partner frequents.

Keeping score. Keeping tabs on how long our partner took to reply and taking as long, if not longer, to respond.

Apologizing for things we haven't done. This one is rooted deep in childhood where we always felt we must have done something wrong if our parents didn't stay connected with us.

Pressuring our partner to keep talking until connection is reestablished. This can take the form of all-night conversations until resolution comes.

Refusing to make the first move to make up. At first glance, this appears to be the opposite of getting back in connection, but it is an attempt to get our partner to prove his or her love by wanting to make up.

If none of these is sufficient to calm the fire in our nervous system, the attempts to bring our partner back often escalate in what are called *protest behaviors*. These are the desperate attempts of a distraught child to find some way to maintain contact, even though these behaviors almost always push our partner further away.

Empty threats. Threatening to leave if our partner doesn't give us what we want.

Angry blaming. Using guilt to get our partner to stay.

Tantrums. Little Me acting out with an angry, physical meltdown.

Internet stalking. Analyzing our partner's likes and follows on Instagram. Obsessively watching their TikTok videos or combing through their Facebook account.

Cheating. Having an affair to make our partner jealous.

You may have other behaviors designed to control the relationship to add to this list. If you recognize yourself in any of the above behaviors, please don't beat yourself up about it. Remember, in infancy, you likely learned that in order to get your needs met, you needed to turn up the volume and expand your energy. You may have screamed to exhaustion to try to get a parent to pick you up. This is simply the way your wounded Little Me is attempting to establish safety and connection. If you find yourself being pulled toward any of these activating strategies or behaviors, the healing work we're dedicated to doing now is going to give you other options. We will be building a foundation of inner security by caring for Little Me and strengthening your Inner Nurturer community. As we do that, your Inner Protectors will soften and your outer protective behaviors will lessen because they will have so much less pain and fear to protect.

From here, you can begin to sense if this is a relationship in which the two of you can work together to help each other heal and grow, or if it is time to move on. All of this is a process, and I know from experience that some days I am more able to access this self-full state than other days. Part of being self-full is being kind to ourselves when we feel half-empty.

Meanwhile, our avoidant partners are dealing with their own internal need for safety. Not having had much emotional connection or soothing as children, they arrive in adulthood with the inner certainty that relationships hold mostly pain. It is better to be independent. At the same time, like all humans, they also long for closeness. As they move toward intimacy, the pain of childhood threatens to break through and they begin to protect themselves, often without realizing that's what's happening. Then they tell themselves stories about why this relationship isn't for them. As their anxious partners begin to feel the first signs of pulling away, they begin their frantic attempts to bring their partners back. How do our avoidant partners behave when we deploy our activating strategies? Generally, some version of withdrawing even further because that is the only way they know to feel safe. We could call these *deactivating strategies* and here are a few of them.

Not calling or texting back. We don't hear from them for a few days, even after a flirty text session or an amazing date.

Not committing or saying "I love you." They withhold information about how they feel about us and the relationship.

Being vague when talking about the future. Even when things are going well, they are unwilling to make concrete plans.

Keeping physical distance. They are unaffectionate, don't like to sleep over, and are unwilling to consider living together even after we've been together for a period of time.

Working or traveling a lot. They use work and travel as a way to keep actual space.

This further agitates us, and we may begin protest behaviors that stimulate our avoidant partners to escalate in their own ways, what we might call *elimination behaviors.*

Pointing out our flaws, including calling us needy. Less about us, this is a way to remind themselves that there are good reasons for not getting close.

Could have affairs. Whether physical or emotional, pursuing intimate connections with other people creates distance and weakens the bond between the two of us. It also insulates these partners from the threat of putting all their eggs in one basket.

Breaking up with us. It comes out of the blue, and at a time when we assumed things were going well. This can make an anxious person crazy trying to figure out what went wrong or, even worse, what we might have done wrong.

Ghosting us. A relatively new way of simply disappearing from our life with no explanation or warning.

Again, you may be able to add other behaviors to this list. While many of the above behaviors hurt us, perhaps we can remember that this is protection mode for avoidant people. This does not excuse their actions or make them okay, but it may allow us to bring some compassion to the situation, which is actually calming for our own ANS. On the flip side, as you can imagine, the deactivating and elimination strategies described above light up an anxious person in a visceral and primal way. The stage is now set for a dramatic back-and-forth that can be as familiar and addictive as it is ultimately devastating. The illustration on the next page shows how the anxious system is activated by the octopus that is reaching out in fear while the avoidant person is "turtling in" when they experience fear.

In some relationships, the constant fear states of the ANS never allow for steady connection, co-regulation, or repair, so the relationship is a roller-coaster ride that feels constantly destabilizing to both partners. However, in chapter 8 we will work on how the octopus energy can learn to soothe the ANS and the turtle can stick its neck out to be more vulnerable in the relationship that provides enough connection and awareness to heal.

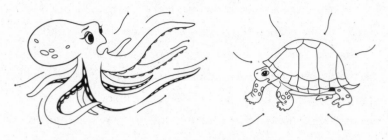

The octopus shows a fear state in an expansion of energy when the ANS is activated. The turtle shows a contraction of energy when the ANS is frightened. Both systems are responding in fear and causing each other to stay in a reactive cycle. It does not matter who starts the cycle, no one can help it, but the responses set off mutual alarms in both people's ANS.

PETER AND LAUREN

Lauren was an attractive thirty-two-year-old client of mine. She had always been anxious, but her attachment wounds never got fully activated until she fell in love with Peter. I believe he tried to love her to the best of his ability. But over time, she began to notice how he would pull away and sometimes even break up with her any time she felt like they were getting closer. She began to experience physical and emotional symptoms related to her anxiety, such as irritable bowel syndrome and obsessive thoughts. Because her childhood had been filled with intensity as she tried to manage her mother's big emotions, she interpreted the strength of her reactions to his coming and going as a sign of true love. For her, intensity equaled love.

When they came in to see me, it was clear that Peter was invested in the relationship. Lauren opened up about her childhood during our sessions, sharing some stories about feeling deeply rejected by her mother no matter how much she concentrated on pleasing her. She had come to believe her mom had never really wanted her. I noticed that Peter was struggling to feel empathy for Lauren in these moments. When I asked him about this, he shared that he found it harder to connect to her when she was vulnerable. He loved the fun-loving, independent Lauren he'd first met, and when she expressed neediness or showed weakness or intense emotions, that was a turnoff. Peter was able to share that in childhood he was punished for being afraid or sad. "Straighten up and act like a man," he remembered his father saying when he was as young as three. The look of disgust on his father's face made Peter sick to his stomach and avoidant of anyone having tender and vulnerable feelings. When we tried to work through these issues, Peter would get upset, literally breaking out in hives and struggling with a strong desire to call off the relationship with Lauren. If dealing with these old excruciating wounds was the price of the relationship, he was ready to leave. Instead of being able to help his Little Me, he protected himself by worrying that Lauren was too needy and that this was a sign she wasn't as smart as he was.

While Peter was able to understand that a lot of his responses were protections at work, his fear of his inner world led him to focus on Lauren's flaws, building a case against her in his head any time they got closer to real intimacy. His body also shut down to the point that he sometimes fell asleep because he could not handle the feelings inside. He remembered doing this as a child, going into his closet for hours at a time to escape his father's scorn. For her part, Lauren fell back into her childhood patterns with her mother, believing that she needed to fix herself in order to make him love her. It never worked with her mom and couldn't work here, either. As her anxiety increased, she started losing weight and having trouble sleeping. It was so sad to see how much they both wanted to figure out how to be together but were held helplessly in the grip of the wounds from very early in life. Just as we can co-regulate in healthy relationships, we also co-dysregulate when neither person can find firm ground within themselves. At each level of desperation, both of them became more entrenched in the old patterns. Over time, Lauren slowly came to accept that the back-and-forth was too traumatic for her. Perhaps sensing the end was near, Peter found somebody else during one of their breakups.

From the outside, it was a sad outcome, as I could see that the connection between them was genuine. Relationships aren't black and white. There were more adult aspects of Lauren and Peter, who had developed a healthy care for each other, but as intimacy increased, they were both thrown back into childhood experiences that meant they were now wounding each other on a daily basis. Ultimately, the most self-full thing Lauren could do in this scenario was move on, with her Little Me and community of Inner Nurturers showing her some areas that needed healing. She was also learning some important lessons about what she actually needs in a partner.

Sometimes a relationship with an extremely avoidant person can light up your attachment system in a way you haven't experienced before. By touching childhood wounds, the intensity of those early needs rises to the surface and, coupled with whatever genuine affection is there, lights a neurochemical fire that feels compelling, enchanting, and even intoxicating. As we do the work of becoming self-full, we are less likely to attract these kinds of partners. And even if we do, our greater clarity in a solid sense of self and easier access to the voice of our Inner Nurturer helps us get out sooner. In Lauren's case, the hardest thing was accepting that her intense attraction and love for Peter were not enough. Each of us wants so much for our love to be received by another person, but she gradually came to understand that nobody was at fault. Their mutual woundedness simply left them with such conflicting needs for reassurance and independence that it was impossible for them to form a stable and mutually beneficial relationship. Both of them needed to do a lot of healing *on their own* before they could be available to each other.

If you are in love with someone who doesn't love you back the way you need and loving them *more* only results in you completely losing yourself, the most profound lesson lies in letting go and realizing that love alone is not enough. So many of us find ourselves in relationships that don't provide a safe haven in which to heal. Instead, they only re-create a destructive cycle of emotional pain. Lauren started to understand why she had become selfless in this dynamic. Her personal growth came from choosing to move forward from a relationship that was filled with turmoil. It was the only path back to herself.

Those of us who are anxiously attached have a particular vulnerability. *Everybody could feel a little bit avoidant to us.* Some people's protections have a tinge of avoidance in them because that's how they learned to protect themselves on occasion. It isn't a predominant feature of how they relate but crops up from time to time. Even this much of a tendency to pull back can activate us. This is what makes it so important to begin the healing practices for Little Me's core wounds and then make them lifelong practices. As long as our Little Me is caught in old pain and fear, we will always see with eyes that are colored by these earlier losses. Even the most well-adjusted people shut down, forget to call back, and need their own space sometimes, acting like the turtle. This means there's a chance we will also have to learn to work with our anxiety in relationships with people who are fundamentally secure but might have turtle protections. However, these relationships will be more forgiving and less taxing for our ANS as a more secure partner will be better able to come back into connection quickly. Over time, these interactions become part of our healing, and our partner's voice and actions part of our Inner Nurturer community. This in itself is part of learning about a kind of love where each partner is allowed to express his or her needs and experience having them met. We will explore this in detail in chapter 8.

ON THE WAY TO EARNING SECURE ATTACHMENT

As we work toward healing, we might not call ourselves *anxiously attached* anymore. We are becoming what is termed *earned secure* in our attachment patterns. It is called this because we didn't get this inner sense of security from our early caregivers, but through our own hard work as adults. Still, for anybody who has ever identified as anxiously attached, when somebody is unavailable for whatever reason, we will likely still be sensitive to their pulling back. It is like feeling the scar tissue from the earlier injury. We will know we are moving into more healing when we have a different response to the old feelings arising. Now, we recognize their origin, and no longer have to act on them in the same dramatically protective ways.

In the midst of our healing, we may find that we are still quite attracted to the challenge and the excitement of the chase because it matches the sympathetic activation in our ANS from childhood experiences. At the same time, the person not "being there" for us confirms what our wounded Little Me knows deep down to be true: *I am not worthy of love, attention, and support.*

This leaves us vulnerable to the common or garden-variety "bad boy." Macho, independent, emotionally unavailable, and totally obsession-worthy, it's likely there have been a few of these types in your past. They have probably left you feeling frustrated and heartbroken by their apparent nonchalance in the face of your burning need for reassurance and connection. Deep trust and intimacy are impossible in these conditions. At some point, the thrill of the chase wears off, and you are left feeling exhausted, confused, and used. Trust me, we have all been there.

With healing, the allure lessens. We are learning to acknowledge what we actually need in a relationship: a high level of connection and a secure, stable attachment. The more comfortable we are about owning this, the less likely we will be to settle for anything less. We are simultaneously learning to recognize the red flags when we see them. This means we will no longer be so quick to fall for what *looks* like "true love" but be drawn to something that *feels* very different, more satisfying and settling. For many of us, there seems to be a middle stage where the nice guys we meet don't bring this rush and can feel boring, even when we can actually see that they are offering the sustained connection we've craved.

We find ourselves asking, "What about the grand romantic gestures, the racing heart, and the butterflies in our stomach? I miss that!" Remember, when we were anxiously attached, these symptoms, which often got mistaken for chemistry, were actually early signs that our attachment wound was being awakened. Again, it's time to get really real with ourselves about what we actually need in a partner if what we are looking for is lasting connection and genuine intimacy: *safety*. And if we think that safe isn't exactly sexy, here's why that isn't true.

It's actually only when we feel safe in a relationship that we develop trust. Once mutual trust has been established, both partners are free to explore the world outside the relationship, where each is able to develop their own interests and replenish their own energy. This creates a healthy foundation and chemistry between two individuals, as each partner is continually bringing something new and different to the relationship, as they evolve and grow together.

This isn't always an easy transition because our systems are so used to the charge of sympathetic arousal. At first, the lack of charge can feel like boredom, but the more time we spend with friends whose ventral system is strong and the more we attune to the needs of Little Me, these trustworthy partners will feel like such a good match for the self-full person we are becoming. The opposite of boring, the safety that allows for this level of autonomy and exploration is what prevents things from becoming stale. If the bad boy or unavailable guy keeps things interesting by constantly keeping you on your toes, the nice guy does it by helping you feel secure enough to keep evolving and growing while the two of you experience the gift of deepening intimacy.

WHEN LACK OF EMPATHY BECOMES ABUSE AND ATTRACTION BECOMES LOVE ADDICTION

Having a partner with strong avoidant protections is one thing, but anxious, empathetic, and selfless people are also at risk of attracting those who thrive on the urgent need to be put on a pedestal: narcissists. How to spot a narcissist? The early attachment wounds in narcissists make them both self-focused and lacking in empathy. Filled with shame and secretly certain they are worth nothing, they protect themselves by consciously believing they are superior to others, thus requiring constant proof of that by insisting on everyone's adoration. In the beginning, to secure our devotion, they also seem to know exactly how to attune to our needs, and have an uncanny knack for making a potential partner feel "special." Imagine how alluring this would be for us when we didn't have that feeling when we were small. The magic radar that draws people together helps narcissists tune in to those of us who will succumb to the seductive bait of specialness.

They are actually practicing an extreme form of self-protection, seeking to control the flow of adoration from us to them. As long as this stays in place, it means never having to be vulnerable to the shame that lurks just under the surface. Since we are all human beings, there is no way to keep feeding this constant need for adoration (although in our selflessness, we will try), so they find something wrong when there is any lapse in idolizing them. This justifies them actively rejecting us. While we are actually fortunate if we are cast away, the anguish it causes deepens the wound inside us and can make us even more vulnerable to another narcissist's wooing of us.

Unfortunately, the tale of the narcissist and the empath is a common one. When people are selfless, they become so other-focused they are likely to attract the opposite: somebody who is selfish or self-centered in the extreme. In this dynamic, selflessness can tip into pathological caretaking where being hypervigilant to the needs of another is the price for staying in the relationship. Narcissists actually create destabilizing scenarios that mean they remain the center of attention, bolstering the belief of their wounded Little Me that they will only get what they need by dominating others. They do this by dishing out little hits of dopamine in the form of attention, a tactic that keeps the empath even more hooked by a process known as *intermittent reinforcement*. This means we stay, waiting for that next moment of focus on us, never knowing when it will come. The modern dating culture can refer to this type of behavior as *breadcrumbing*, when your partner shows interest just to keep you hooked during those moments they sense they're losing you. It can make you feel like you're on a lousy roller-coaster ride. Even talking about this may stir up the sensations of sympathetic activation right now.

This kind of dynamic can actually be dangerous for somebody who is anxiously attached because staying in a relationship with a narcissist can border on a form of self-harm. The selfless person will give endlessly of themselves, to the extent that they almost disappear, while becoming ever more anxious. There are no moments of safety and true connection because narcissists are so intent on their own complete lack of safety. Shame is always threatening to break through. Narcissists must keep feeding on the feeling of being adored, becoming upset and angry (and possibly violent) any time they cease being made to feel "special." Inside, both people are desperate children caught in a dance that only causes more wounding, but we are the ones taking the brunt of punishment on the outside. Why do we stay? When we are anxiously attached, we believe that "being needed" is the same as "being loved," so it is understandable the extent to which we will take on responsibility for caretaking a narcissistic partner's agonized wounded child. Often, the more closely the wound in our parents resembles the wound in the narcissist, the more difficult it will be for us to leave the relationship.

Do you think you might have been snared by a narcissist? While it's a term that gets thrown around a lot, full-blown narcissistic personality disorder in fact only affects approximately 0.5 to 5 percent of the general population (with a greater prevalence in men). But there are varying degrees to which narcissistic tendencies may be expressed, and anybody who falls on the spectrum of self-focused and lacking in empathy may display some of them. Most of us have moments like this. When we are sufficiently threatened, even if we are mostly selfless, we will turn toward actions that are solely focused on getting what we need to feel safe.

As with everybody, this is not the narcissist's fault. These traits are the result of how they learned to protect themselves in the face of being repeatedly shamed and humiliated in early childhood. But if you do suspect your avoidant partner of having narcissistic tendencies, no amount of bending over backward for them will lead to a loving partnership with a personality this extreme. Being in true connection with another would bring on a degree of vulnerability that would threaten to push them into the intolerable pool of shame. Imagine the desperation of a drowning person and you can get the feeling of what it is like to be a narcissist who is threatened with exposure to his or her inner world. At the same time, every brick you build in the wall of your own self-regard is felt as a threat to their survival, so they will be there waiting with another put-down or dismissive act to tear you down. The only course of action in this scenario is to first recognize and accept what is happening, and then to walk away. If one of the purposes of every relationship is to help us learn something about ourselves, the lesson learned in this case is that loving someone more and trying harder to get them to love you does not always get the two of you to the mutuality of a healthy relationship. Such a change requires both people to do the hard work of healing, and for most narcissists, the amount of pain they would face keeps them locked into behaviors that make sure this will never happen.

Even though we "know" we need to walk away, we will not always be able to do that. An anxious person's response to the intensity and desperation of their narcissistic partner may be to step beyond codependency and fall into love addiction. An addiction is something we repetitively do to protect us from feeling old pain and fear. While it temporarily comforts the wound, it doesn't *heal* it, so we always need more—another "fix." Just like any other drug, the feel-good chemicals of first love can quickly create their own kind of dependency, especially for someone who is anxiously attached. The neurochemicals that get released in the early phase of relationships feel extra potent because as children we did not receive enough of them, so our reaction when we feel them release is heightened.

In the grip of love addiction, our focus narrows until nothing else matters. All we can think about is finding and keeping a partner who will satisfy our craving for love. This urgent need is what keeps us coming back for more, even when we logically know the relationship is not good for us. When we get to this point, we're in danger of losing ourselves entirely in the search for love's momentary soothing. We are a perfect match for the narcissist's need for a constantly adoring person who will endlessly provide worshipful attention, no matter how damaging to us. While love addiction can be as hard to kick as a powerful narcotic, it's also a by-product of your Little Me, your inner wounded child who we met in chapter 2, searching for somebody to "fix" or fill up what feels broken and empty inside. So there is hope.

What is going on within our system when we find ourselves captured by love addiction? First of all, not only is it normal to crave a relationship with a loving partner, it's equally normal to devote a lot of time to him or her in the beginning. You're in love and your partner is all you can think about. It becomes hard to focus on work, and this person is all you talk about to your friends. You obsess over his or her social media feeds and want to spend all of your time with her or him, hanging on their every word. You even begin to start looking into summer versus fall weddings. While it feels like this one is the source of all these crazy-good feelings, it's actually your own body chemistry that's fueling this dance.

In the very early stages of a new love, we are literally "high" on a cocktail of neurochemicals and hormones designed to help us form an attachment with this person. First of all, dopamine (which is also released when a person consumes alcohol or drugs like heroin and cocaine) creates a sense of seeking and newness when we're with them, while also making them seem exciting and special. Simply put, we can't get enough. Next up, norepinephrine floods our system with energy, with an effect like being on amphetamines. We can't eat, we can't sleep, and we mistake our racing heart for a sign of true love. And finally, our body experiences a significant drop in mood-regulating serotonin, making us more likely to obsess about our new partner. This person becomes all we can think about, and we start coming up with ways we should change to fit in with what we perceive as her or his needs.

The combined effect of these three chemicals makes forging a new and meaningful connection with another person one of the most pleasurable and satisfying human experiences, up there with mind-blowing sex (which we're probably also having) or winning the lottery. It makes sense that it's easy to become *addicted* to this feeling. Who wouldn't want to feel like the luckiest person in the world every day?

But what goes up must come down, and this initial rush of feel-good chemicals isn't going to last. A natural transition is trying to happen as a couple moves from constant seeking to feeling a trusting, ongoing bond with each other. Once that first feeling wears off (which can take weeks, months, or even years in the case of some couples), our system wants to settle into a more sustainable pattern. As a relationship moves into the realm of lasting attachment, oxytocin, the "cuddle hormone" that's also released during orgasm, childbirth, and breastfeeding, helps us form the trust necessary for monogamous bonds. This is a natural and necessary next step in bonding with a partner over the long term, but it can feel like an earth-shattering comedown for somebody who needs the intensity a baby feels with his or her mother because that need was never fulfilled.

For those of us whose injuries leave us most vulnerable to love addiction, that initial high feels so good and so absolutely necessary that it can easily be mistaken for the answer to our prayers, even though we are handing over our power in exchange for all these potent and exciting feelings. The chemicals combine to give us the sensation of having met somebody who is madly in love with us and seems to know instinctively how to fulfill our emotional needs. This sounds exactly like what happens between parents and a new baby who are forming a secure bond. Meanwhile, the restless energy of the norepinephrine puts us on high alert for the first signs that they may be pulling away. Coupled with a drop in serotonin, we have more difficulty settling and begin to obsess about his or her every move until we can't think about anything else. The responses of a narcissistic partner only intensify this process with their ongoing behaviors to keep us feeding their wounds. Before we know it, a biological process designed to help us form a lasting attachment is actually stirring up our deepest fears of abandonment, seeded in our early relationships. Deep down inside, our wounded Little Me is being called up, while back in the relationship, we begin to modify our behavior to try to keep getting even the most momentary infusion of this love cocktail.

Both the narcissist and the love addict are in the grip of childhood wounds so severe that they are not in control of their responses to each other. It is a blessing when the relationship breaks apart, as there is virtually no hope for healing such wounds within the relationship. Love addicts often need support in leaving, but then the door is open to taking steps toward healing.

The main difference between people with an avoidant attachment style and pathological narcissists is that the former often have the ability to look at their behaviors and take responsibility for their part. Their wounds aren't so deep that it makes it impossible to do that. Many avoidant people can also feel empathy and vulnerability. They just have a very different way of expressing this, protecting themselves so that their responses feel cold and callous because the softer emotions were neither acceptable nor modeled for them in their families. This was the situation with Lauren and Peter, who couldn't find their way through their difficulties to lasting partnership. However, it is also true that many avoidant people will be able to get the help they need to heal these old wounds. Often, this can happen in couples therapy as both people in the anxious-avoidant couple get the support they need to heal their core wounds together. I have seen people invested in this work come out the other side with a greater depth of caring, understanding, and empathy than many couples who started from a healthier place. This is very good news indeed.

♥♥

FIRST STEPS TOWARD HEALING

We're just about to begin the journey back to our selves. Perhaps we can picture our body as a home, one that has the potential to be a sanctuary for us. A place to be quiet, to feel at ease, to get deeply in touch with our wounds and our needs. But for anybody who has experienced trauma, including emotional neglect, being fully in our body often feels unsafe. We may even have served our selves an eviction notice as a form of self-protection, finding it hard to sit and simply be. Reconnecting with our body awareness is an important part of the process of becoming self-full.

As we have learned, our earliest experiences create different sensations and feelings in our bodies, which send messages to our brains. From these sensations, we form narratives about the safety of the world around us and how people will relate with us. These nervous system patterns also guide our responses to certain current-day experiences. If it was safer to not be in our bodies as children, our response now may be to become "disembodied." If we can't sense stress, pain, or fear, we'll feel safer detaching from our feelings. This is often how the body of an avoidantly attached person protects itself from feelings of annihilation. On the other hand, an anxiously attached person is often very sensitive, most of all to the feelings and thoughts of the other person, losing track of his or her own because our safety rests with managing the feelings and behaviors of others. To really feel at home within our selves, so we no longer crave the escape into another, we must gather the courage to drop back down into the body. To feel it *all*. Everything starts here, and so we must cultivate the practice of *inner attunement*. Along with forming a cognitive and emotional awareness of our core wounds and how they get activated, an embodied awareness is a vital part of changing the deeply held responses that get us trapped in love addiction and codependency.

As we move through part two of this book, I will accompany you back home into your body, where we will find a rich array of feelings held by different ego states jostling for attention inside of you. This awareness of both the body and the internal states that cause your external reactions is key to integrating what you are feeling with what you are thinking. It will help you understand what is happening in your body and your ANS when your anxious attachment system is activated. If this sounds daunting, I want you to know what a rock star you are for choosing to do this work. Taking the time to come home to yourself is laying the foundation for a whole new way of relating to yourself and others. It is how you develop an unshakable sense of safety in the very depths of your being.

2

Becoming
Self-Full

CHAPTER 4

Listen to Your Heart

Now it's time for us to begin the real work of becoming self-full, which means learning how to access the deepest parts of our selves. This journey into the vast, unknown territory of your inner world can bring up many complicated feelings but can also be a fascinating and exciting adventure. It is vital, therefore, that you feel safe, loved, and supported before you go in. That is why we do this together. Because the world of an anxious person didn't offer resources for emotional safety and connection, even if there was love, and it is important to have those. Now you may also have others in your life—a therapist and trustworthy friends—who can be part of this safety net for the journey.

If you are anxiously attached, becoming self-full means being supported so you can establish a more loving relationship to your self. I'm going to guide and accompany you to cultivate a safe and compassionate inner environment where you can do this work. This will make it all right for painful feelings to arise and be expressed—a process that requires bravery and radical honesty, which is another essential part of becoming self-full.

In part one, we talked about how for us anxiously attached people, our wounded Little Me takes over in relationships. In order to soothe this younger part of us, we first need to really be in touch with our Little Me and their unmet needs. But they won't just come out and tell us what these are until there is a feeling of safety. Just like with outer children, if our first reaction is to criticize, berate, or even reject them, this side of ourselves will hide away. But when our Little Me sees that we are receptive and accepting of them, they will open up. So it is time to introduce two other players in this inner story: your Inner Protectors (there are often more than one) and your Inner Nurturers (also often more than one). These two parts have a huge influence on your Little Me. Our Inner Protectors are always quick with words of warning, often not delivered gently, and our Inner Nurturers are loving adult or mentor figures who care for every part of us.

Perhaps we're already familiar with the various protective voices inside. Some are critical of us so that we don't do the same behaviors that got us into trouble when we were younger. "Don't complain." "Don't ask for attention." Or voices of doubt. "See? He doesn't really like you." "If your parents didn't love you, why should she?" Or ones who keep our whole focus on the relationship. They often arrive more as a feeling of hypervigilance than in words. If the relationship becomes unbearably painful, they activate the protest behaviors we do as a last resort. Each of us has a unique Protective Team that we will come to know well as we do our work. In this chapter, we'll get to know these three distinct parts of our selves. Together, we can cultivate curiosity about our Protectors as we grow to understand why each of them has their own wisdom, and all of them are there only because the pain and fear we carry needs them.

We'll also begin to meet the community of Inner Nurturers, made up of the internalized presence of all those who have cared for us with attention, understanding, warmth, and steady presence. Because these people touched our heart (which is the third brain in our body), we often feel them right there in our chest. For just a moment, place your hand on your chest and see what feelings arrive. Because we have been talking about Nurturers, we may find someone who has cared for us arises in our minds. Or because the heart-brain is part of where we store memories of connection, someone who has hurt us through painful connection or abandoned us might come to mind. For now, it is helpful to notice how deeply we have taken in the people in our lives who have mattered to us.

Most of us haven't thought of our heart as a brain, but more a metaphor for romantic love in all its forms. New research is showing that there is a lot more to this organ than we thought—and that it has its own kind of intelligence. The HeartMath Institute is an organization that researches how people can bring their physical, mental, and emotional systems into balanced alignment with their heart's intuitive guidance. Their research shows that the heart-brain (the intrinsic cardiac nervous system) is *equally* as smart as the brain in our skull and belly.

This heart-brain is made up of neurotransmitters, support cells, proteins, and ganglia—all complex and intricate—much like the information networks of the head-brain. It is also believed that the heart-brain is strongly tied together with the head-brain, constantly sending messages that affect how we think, feel, behave, and relate. In fact, about eighty percent of the communication flows upward and only twenty percent flows downward from the brain in our skull. That's a very substantial flow of information shaping our feelings and what we do next. Because it communicates via neurotransmitters and sensations, we mostly don't consciously hear its messages.

This means that a big part of understanding our selves and healing our emotional lives, including our romantic relationships, is about being able to listen to our hearts' messages. This will help us balance what we *know* in our heads with what we *feel* in our hearts. Our heads are filled with the beliefs that have come from our core wounds. How often we find our Protectors mulling things over, playing out scenarios, planning next steps to secure the relationship. Heart intelligence, rooted in the caring relationships we have had and experienced as the community of Nurturers, is a source of intuitive guidance and knowledge that goes beyond the logical brain. Part of that wisdom is that through cultivating awareness of the heart's messages, we can also come into contact with the pain that has come from broken connections. As we do this, the door to healing opens.

The path to relieving the pain of our core wounds is to acknowledge that they still hurt and to allow ourselves to feel them fully so we can receive the warm care of another right at the root of the wound. As we move through the pain with support, we will reach a place on the other side that feels calm, wholesome, and secure.

This can only happen once we start honoring the feelings stored within our heart—perhaps we need to grieve or get furious—before they can receive the reparative experience that can heal even the oldest, most painful wounds.

When we listen from our heart, the logical division of the brain tends to soften and dissolve, which enables us to access the interconnectedness beneath the divisions and categories that prevent us from accessing our own wisdom. We begin to experience that just as the heart underlies the brain; this interconnectedness underlies everything. When your heart starts to find its way back to warm, connected feelings and enters a state of openness, or coherence, with your brain, your nervous system responds by increasing the brain's energy, creativity, and intuition, allowing for a strong connection between your heart and your brain and adding to the feelings of wholeness.

Before we begin, it's really important that you take your time with this work. We will be moving into deeper connection to our intuitive selves, developing full-body awareness. The fancy word for this is *interoception*. When we cultivate this capacity, we will have *felt sense*, which is a bodily knowing inside of us that allows access to all the parts of us that have experienced warmth and goodness (our Inner Nurturers), those parts that work every day to keep us safe (our Inner Protectors), as well as the parts that carry the pain and fear that needs healing (Little Me in their many aspects). The first step is to be sure you have others to support you. I can be one of them. I have recorded the practices we are going to do so my voice (and my heart) can accompany you through the process. It is important to keep asking yourself if you need additional support. Our culture tends to encourage us to go it alone, so checking in regularly to see what your system is asking for is very important. When we feel old feelings, it is often as if we are experiencing them right *now*. This can be an overwhelming process, especially if there is trauma stored in your body. For this reason, it is very important that you go at your own pace and set up a safe environment in which to do this work.

Please go slowly and be kind to yourself as you go inward. If you begin experiencing anxiety, racing thoughts, or feeling frozen or "zoned out," it's a sign that it's time to shift gears and get back into the present. Any time you feel overwhelmed, I want you to pause the work, put the book down, and find a place to sit where you can plant your feet on the ground, ideally with your shoes off. Open your eyes and notice the details in your immediate environment. Focus on your breath and label some of the things you are seeing, speaking out loud to yourself. Put your hands on the chair, and notice any noises or scents in the air. I like to keep flowers in my office when I'm doing this work with clients, as looking at something beautiful can help bring you quickly back into the present. Visualizing the eyes of a loved one can also help you feel connected to warmth and safety.

Right at the beginning of this process, you can also let a friend know that you are going to be doing some inner work and that you may need to call them if things get intense. Make it somebody you feel completely safe with and who you know will be supportive of your process. If you work with a therapist, you can also share this work with them, and even bring it into your sessions if that feels good. And if all this sounds daunting, please acknowledge the fear and then reach out for a hand to hold. Becoming self-full is a process that will become easier with time and practice. Your sense of inner safety and support will expand as we move through this, layer by layer. Lastly, before we begin, please set an intention for yourself—which is a statement you can repeat to yourself to help you connect to the energy you want to tap into. It might be something like: "I am learning safe new ways to experience my inner world, which will allow me to experience true love." And, above all, please remember that I am right here with you.

♥

EXERCISE:
BEGINNING TO LISTEN TO OUR HEARTS

Before we dive into a guided meditation to bring your awareness deeply into your heart intelligence, I want to offer some ways to become more "heart aware" every day. We're not used to communicating with this part of our selves, so don't expect to get it right away. The aim is simply to learn how to listen more closely to your heart. This five-step process is one way to begin.

1. In small moments throughout your day, notice how you're feeling. Just ask yourself, "How am I feeling right now?" Place your awareness in your chest area and try to allow your heart—rather than your head—to answer. Be aware of any sensations and emotions that come up in response, but don't try to analyze them. For now, simply cultivate the habit of checking in with your heart.

2. When you check with what you are sensing inside your heart, also sense the quality of your breath. The way we breathe— whether calm, rushed, deep, or shallow—can tell us a lot about what's going on below the surface of our thinking minds.

3. If you notice over time that your breathing is most often shallow and quick, explore what it feels like to extend your breaths. Breathe in while counting to five, breathe out while counting to seven. Imagine that your breath is going all the way down into your belly and spreading 360 degrees, so that your stomach softly expands and contracts with each breath rather than your chest. Now check in again with what you sense and feel. Can you access your emotional state more easily?

4. Check your posture. Are your shoulders hunched around your chest, your arms crossed? If so, try rolling your shoulders back so that you are standing or sitting a little straighter. This will create more space around your heart. After doing this, check in with yourself again and notice any changes in the way you feel.

5. As a final step, imagine that your breath is collecting in your lungs, filling up in all directions as it washes over your heart, cleansing it and making space for it to open. Again, notice if you are more connected to how you feel.

The more you practice this awareness exercise, the more your heart will begin speaking to you. As you slowly open to the Inner

Nurturers who embody your heart's intelligence, you will also notice that they communicate differently than the way your brain does, mostly through sensation, which is the language of the body. Whatever message comes through, your job for now is simply to accept it. This is not about "fixing" any feelings or emotions that arise, but rather just letting them be. Over time, with practice, you may begin to find yourself checking in with your heart, your breath, and your posture as routinely as brushing your teeth.

When you feel inspired and ready to connect more deeply with your heart, read through this next exercise. You can download a recorded audio version of this exercise at **beselffull.com/meditations** and listen to the guided meditation. Before you press play, sense that we can do this together, invoke your curiosity, take courage, and get ready to explore the next frontier of your heart's intelligence.

EXERCISE:
HEART SCAN MEDITATION

Please go slowly the first time you do this exercise. Then, once you learn how to do the Heart Scan, you can drop in at any time and complete it in a few minutes. The Heart Scan is a powerful way to tune in to yourself on a physical, energetic, and emotional level. Practicing it will help you cultivate the safe, loving, and supportive inner world where you will do the work of becoming self-full. It was created by a dear friend and colleague of mine, Lynn Carroll. Lynn is a wonderful therapist who guides her clients into deeper connection with their selves by cultivating body awareness. With her Heart Scan Meditation, you can tune in to what your heart is saying at any given moment.

1. Start by finding a quiet place where you feel comfortable and protected. The Heart Scan can be done in any environment, but to start, it's helpful to practice in a space where you feel physically safe.

2. Tell yourself that it is time to slow down. This inner cue will help you shift gears from whatever you were doing before to the quiet place where you want to be. Consciously slow your pace until you can truly connect with what is happening within your body. Slow your breathing, slow your movements.

3. Close your eyes and breathe slowly and gently as you bring awareness to your heart center, in the middle of your chest. Tune in and observe. Does your heart feel open, closed, or neutral? You're probably not used to describing your experiences or feelings from a sensory perspective or using sensory language. Some examples of sensory experiences you might have when feeling your heart center include tension, tingling sensations, spaciousness, hardness, denseness, blankness, light, expansiveness, or heaviness. What do you feel? Just observe. Notice if you feel anxiety, peacefulness, or neutrality. Sometimes all of these can be present simultaneously. Simply be with whatever is.

4. As you bring awareness to your heart, you may see images or colors and feel strong emotions. Thoughts, fears, or old memories may arise. Simply observe and notice what happens in your body. As you become more aware, see if your body settles more or becomes more tense.

5. Whatever comes up, go with the flow. We are always changing, from moment to moment. If you feel your thoughts speeding up, tension building, or even a sense of becoming overwhelmed, bring your attention back to your breath. Focusing on the breath for a time can help settle your system and relax you.

6. Continue to name what you're noticing without getting attached to any specific thought or sensation. Just name things, like "shoulder tension," "sadness," "peace," "worry," "impatience," "sleepiness." Allow yourself to go with the moment. What is it like to look more objectively at your experience, to feel the sensations in your body, and notice what your heart center feels like? Perhaps you are beginning to get a sense of how this form of intelligence is different from *thinking*.

7. Now allow an image to emerge that gives you a sense of peace. Maybe it's walking in the mountains or on a beach, playing with your pet, or when you're baking or reading. Whatever image comes in, allow yourself to be present with what feels good. What happens in your body? How do you know it feels

comfortable? What emotions come up in your heart? Notice any images that arise and just observe what happens in your heart center when you evoke a sense of peace.

8. Now think of a time when you felt loved. You may draw from an early childhood memory or from a more recent experience. If you believe that you haven't felt loved, imagine what being loved would feel like. When you see this image of feeling loved, notice what happens in your heart. Does your heart feel warm, lighter, more open? Does it start to close down? What thoughts are you conscious of as you imagine being loved? Let them arise, and then let them go.

9. Expand your awareness beyond your heart center. What sensations are you feeling throughout your body? Which emotions are present? If your thinking mind starts to speed up, pay attention to feeling the sensations in your body. Start with your in-breath and out-breath, noticing how they feel.

10. If your body feels empty, blank, or if there is a wall or source of separation, become curious about these sensations. Do you see the colors of the wall? How thick is the barrier? As you sit with it, does it change? What does it remind you of? Do any memories come up? Just notice what happens inside.

11. If you feel stuck, notice where you feel it. Allow it to be there. What does it feel like, look like? Does paying attention to it instead of resisting it cause it to shift? Ask your heart intel-

ligence what you can give yourself to feel unstuck. Then imagine yourself receiving it.

12. Bring your attention back to your heart center. Can you keep your focus there? Or do you find you are constantly pulled outside of your self, wondering what others are saying or doing, thinking about work, mulling over the past or planning your day tomorrow? Maybe you observe that you don't want to be present with the emotions in your heart. Maybe you're not ready.

13. As you continue to listen to your heart, it may show you what it needs from you to feel safer, more open, more loving, more accepting. These may appear as images or simply intuitive "knowings." Notice how tuning in to your heart on a deep level allows you to receive messages from your inner world.

When you learn to become present with your heart in this way, no matter what is happening within or without, you will learn with practice and time to feel more connected to a true source of safety, love, and support. Sometimes these will come as feelings and sensations, sometimes as the sense of the inner presence of someone who has cared for us, an Inner Nurturer. We'll revisit this Heart Scan Meditation in chapter 8 when you begin exploring how to stay heart-centered in your relationships. For now, get to know your heart by doing this exercise in a variety of situations, so that you learn now to access your heart's intelligence whenever you need it. This will be a theme we will return to throughout our healing journey together, as the heart is the bedrock of the safe, loving, and supportive inner world that will allow you to be with and heal your painful wounds, find emotional balance, and, ultimately, relearn how to love.

BEFRIENDING YOUR INNER PROTECTORS

One goal of this chapter is to help you relate to your Little Me from a loving and supportive place, which means learning how to understand the role of your Inner Protectors. During your Heart Scan Meditations, you may become hyperaware of just how loud and insistent these harsh and critical voices may be at times, often there in the background, quick to suggest that you should or shouldn't do this or that. Just as with your Little Me, they must be fully acknowledged so that they can become part of the healing process.

The transition from wanting to push these Protectors away to feeling grateful for them is one of the most important shifts internally. It's understandable that we want the critical voices to stop, and yet their degree of forcefulness is also a direct indication of how much pain and fear they are trying to shelter from more harm. If my mind is telling me to never, ever ask for someone to notice me, I can be sure that I was so rarely noticed that there is an ocean of pain inside. Each of us can probably think of examples of this in our own lives. So gratitude really is appropriate for every Protector who is guarding the door on behalf of a hurting Little Me. They are trying to make sure that this Little Me doesn't get shamed or criticized for not living up to cultural or family expectations.

But there is another aspect to our Inner Protectors. While not meaning to hold us back, they reinforce the things we fear the most: that we are inadequate, unlovable, too sensitive—all the ways we were seen as unacceptable in our past relationships. Because they stem from fear, they see things strictly in black and white. Good and bad, right and wrong. They stir up anxiety and shame in the name of protecting us, while unintentionally reinforcing all our negative core beliefs. As we befriend them and offer these parts of us compassion, they will often give us access to the Little Me they are protecting. And once the Little Me is healed, these Protectors will not be needed in the same way. This deep inner work with the pain and fear really is the shortcut to stilling the inner voices that haunt us each day.

As we have been talking about Protectors, it's likely one of yours has made an appearance. Notice how they might look and sound in your mind. Maybe it is the voice of one of your parents. One client told me, "I hear my mother counseling me not to win at Ping-Pong or the boys won't like me, so now, every time I want to assert myself in a group of men, my whole body pulls back, my throat tightens so I can't speak. If I try to override it, the loud critical voice shouts at me for being an idiot." It could more abstractly be the voice of society. "It's unladylike/unmanly to [fill in the blank]." One of my male clients said that as much as his wife and daughters loved him, they would rather he died than showed weakness. What are yours saying? Is it possible to listen to them so deeply that you can follow them back to the root of the pain and fear they are working so hard to not have happen again?

The paradox is that listening to this voice often *feels* safe. It seems like they are talking sense. After all, if you're rich and thin, just like all the magazines and the movies say, won't your life be perfect? Unfortunately, no. Having flat abs or a high bank balance has *nothing* to do with your capacity to love and be loved. Until there has been a lot of healing, our Inner Protectors are going to continue because they are driven to try to protect you from more of the same pain you have learned to expect. The inner voice of this Protector can be critical and shaming toward you in hopes of protecting you from those exact feelings in your external world. Without healing, they are an addiction of sorts, compelled to continue their ways until there is less pain and fear to keep away.

When we befriend this part of us, understanding that their role has only ever been to protect Little Me from more pain and thank Little Me for their service, the Protectors begin to feel heard and understood. Trust develops, and they become willing to open the door into the realm where Little Me's pain and fear are held; now the Protectors see us as an ally in keeping Little Me safe rather than somebody intent on further hurting or criticizing this precious child they guard. As these old wounds heal, there is less need for our Inner Protectors to try to stand between Little Me and yet more pain. Their voices quiet as Little Me is more and more able to experience the joys of curiosity, wonder, playfulness, and intuition that are available as Little Me heals. We see that our Inner Protectors are as *equally deserving* of unconditional love as every other part of us. These Protectors gradually shift their focus to providing care and advice that is centered on what is happening in the here and now rather than guarding against a repeat of past pain. Instead of "You shouldn't let anyone see your tears," they may say, "Your tears are valuable. Is this the person you can safely share them with?" Their wise guidance begins to help you discern who may be trustworthy companions for you.

EXERCISE:
HOW YOUR INNER PROTECTORS
BECOME ALLIES

Are you ready to befriend your Inner Protectors? Good. The first step is to become aware of when your Inner Protectors are speaking in your ear. If you're anxiously attached, it's likely their voices have become such a constant in the back of your mind that you even believe they are the strongest part of you. Maybe even the real you. But remember, they are not. An Inner Protector is simply one part of a rich inner world. By consciously identifying them as such, you will become more and more practiced at noticing how they are trying to protect you. They can help you see which parts of yourself you have had to abandon in order to feel accepted. When they say, "Don't you dare speak up to your boss," you may begin to remember how unsafe it was to voice any disagreement in your family. Follow the steps below to get to know your Inner Protectors better:

1. Begin to listen for your Inner Protectors as a conscious practice. The words *should* and *shouldn't* often announce their presence.

2. Gain awareness of the messages they repeat. As you begin to listen closely, do you notice themes? What issues are most important for them? As you develop your ability to observe their patterns, you may also begin to remember times that these very thoughts, feelings, and behaviors were not acceptable at home.

3. Thank your Inner Protectors for helping you not repeat the things that got you into trouble at home. Thank them for helping you open the door to healing these old core wounds. Let them know that you are dedicated to doing that so you will have more freedom to respond differently now. Express confidence that they will be able to be less vigilant as you heal and that you look forward to their helpful guidance in being aware of your impact on others—and vice versa. You may notice your Inner Protectors softening already, just because they are being accepted as a valuable part of you.

As you keep at this, you will sense just how harsh and commanding your Inner Protectors can be. You have paid attention to the Protectors because it seemed that listening to these negative, critical voices would steer you right. You may fear that without them, you will be left with no protection, no self-awareness, and no idea where you're headed in life. It's like being a horse that forgets it can walk without being whipped forward. The truth is that your Inner Protectors will slowly soften when you heal the pain inside and continue to guide you in a gentle way.

Now, let's look again at how your Inner Protectors interact with your Little Me. Remember Susan's story from chapter 2? She was irritated with her partner, Dan, for not helping with the dishes. Her Little Me was feeling angry and unappreciated. But her Inner Protectors were warning, "Don't say anything! You'll only upset him. Speaking your mind will only lead to a fight. He'll probably leave you. It's your job to meet his needs, not his job to meet yours. Your feelings aren't important." These fears were rooted in Susan's core abandonment wound and are an example of how a person's Inner Protectors try to protect Little Me from being abandoned again.

If Susan heeds her Inner Protectors, Little Me will cower and hide. She will push down her anger, and her resentments will build. If her Little Me prevails, she may become emotionally unstable and yell at Dan rather than having a conversation about her feelings and the dishes. Her actions may be driven by emotional impulses that have no guardrails. Those of us who are anxiously attached will be familiar with both these responses. They will continue to play out until caring and reasonable adults, your Inner Nurturers, can intervene and help you begin the healing process. But by understanding what your Inner Protectors are trying to save you from experiencing, you can gain more insight into your core wounds.

MEETING YOUR COMMUNITY OF INNER NURTURERS

No matter how ill-equipped our parents may or may not have been to meet our needs, we all have had other relationships that helped us build an inner community of nurturing people. To help you picture it, I want you to think back—what person in your life has been the most loving, validating, nurturing, and supportive? Even small moments of this kind of connection matter. If that community is small now, the work we are going to do is an opportunity to add the presence of others who will be with us for our lifetime. All of their support doesn't come as words. Because they were truly present to us and reflected our goodness and value, they strengthened our sense of identity as a worthy person and seeded hope that others would come along to treat us the same way. Their comforting and wise presence also helps us navigate even the most painful and difficult emotions, which is what makes it possible to be with our full selves.

In the busyness of our lives and with the anxiety that accompanies our relationships, most of us are not used to connecting to the support of these Inner Nurturers. Instead, our Inner Protectors take center stage to shelter us from as much pain as possible. Now, we are consciously going to start connecting with this community of Nurturers and bringing them into relationship with the Inner Protectors and the aspects of Little Me. As much as possible, we will draw on people you have internalized because they do become living beings who offer ongoing support inside us. They are, without exception, resources of safety, continually co-regulating with us. Below is a list of suggestions to help you conjure up the energy of your Inner Nurturers.

- Certain moments when you felt seen and held and loved by a parent who couldn't always be present

- Your therapist or another coach or mentor figure who sees and reflects you with warmth
- A close and supportive friend who has been a source of acceptance in your life
- A favorite pet who has always been there for you and shown you unconditional love and support
- A teacher who has not only supported your learning but cared for you as a person
- A geographical place where you have felt especially "at home." This could be a place in nature or a physical location where you have felt held and safe

We may also feel profoundly supportive relationships with others with whom we don't have a daily human relationship.

- Famous role models who demonstrate their warmth and compassion through their activities in the world
- A figure from your spiritual tradition—many of us have a relationship with a higher power, whether we call it God, Shakti, the universe, or Mother Nature

Let's take a moment to slowly read these lists again, sensing who spontaneously arises inside us. As we come into contact with these resources within, notice if an Inner Protector also arrives. They might be worried that you're taking your eye off possible threats. Or they might even deny the existence of these people inside. "How do you know they're real? They might be imaginary." It is helpful to acknowledge the Inner Protector. "I hear you. I know you're worried. I want you to get to know these Nurturers, too. We could use the help." As many times as you hear your Protectors' words, offer thanks and go back to your Nurturers. In this way, you're actually beginning to build new neural pathways between these two groups who have usually stayed so separate in your mind and heart. The truth is that we need both protection and nurturance, and that the parts of us that hold the experiences of care and support are needed by the parts of us that are likely exhausted from trying to keep us safe.

EXERCISE:
LISTENING TO OUR NURTURERS

Once you are in touch with someone you have internalized who is the voice and the energy of your Inner Nurturers, spend some time getting to know them. The exercise below is designed to explore this new relationship and to invite this secure and protective energy into your life. Because this feeling of connection arises in the heart, you can also think of it as the voice of your heart intelligence. You can download the exercise as a guided meditation at **beselffull.com /meditations** and do it as often as you like. It might be a lovely way to start each day with whichever Nurturer might want to come in at that moment.

1. Close your eyes and visualize who you chose as your Inner Nurturer for this exercise. As best you can, picture them in

your heart to *feel* their love, warmth, compassion, kindness, and acceptance. Allow all these feelings to flow into you, and notice how this affects you on a sensory, physical level. It may feel so good that you find yourself smiling. You may experience an emotional release and begin to cry. That's okay. Simply rest in the presence of this inner resource and allow whatever comes up.

2. Now ask your Inner Nurturer if they have any messages for you. Listen deeply to hear the response on all levels of your being: whether verbal, emotional, or sensorial. You may hear what sounds like your own voice in your head telling you: "You are safe," or simply feel a sensation of warmth and love. Or perhaps there will be some discomfort, as your Inner Nurturer acknowledges that this exercise is challenging and new for you. And that this is okay.

3. Allow yourself to feel reassured and seen, accepted and encouraged. Safe. What do you notice about yourself through the eyes of this loving presence? What positive sense of yourself is being validated?

4. Trust that you are allowed to experience whatever you are feeling: "empty," "peaceful," "happy," or "sad." Your Inner Nurturer is offering you a safe space. They want you to know that your emotional reality is your reality. They want you to know that it is safe to be you.

5. If an Inner Protector shows up, perhaps shaming you for feeling the way you do, allow your Inner Nurturer to gently intervene. Acknowledge the Protector's suggestion and reassure them that all is well. Hear your Inner Nurturer tell the Inner Protector that you are safe, supported, and loved, and that it's okay for you to be feeling whatever is coming up.

6. Now ask your Inner Nurturer to help you heal your wounded Little Me by offering safety, support, and unconditional love. Invite them to be present for you as you move forward in your life.

7. Thank this loving presence for helping you heal. And thank your Inner Protectors for working so hard to keep you safe. When you are ready, open your eyes.

Now that we are actively engaging these caring ones inside, you may find yourself drawn to them many times in the day. At first, some of my clients have a hard time grasping the idea that we can take someone's love, support, energy, and good intention for us into our inner world. However, I notice that many of my clients naturally begin to say things like "When I'm struggling with not drinking, I hear your voice in my mind." Or "All I have to do is put my hand on my chest, and I feel you right with me." It is such a wonderful thing that our brains are built so that we can take others in to be comforting presences whenever we need that care and support.

You may also hear both your Inner Nurturers and your Inner Protectors in conversation. All of this is rebuilding your world inside in preparation for Little Me to arrive in an environment where they can feel safe. In the next chapter, we will further engage your Inner Nurturers in ways that increase their influence as you learn to lean into their presence to heal your wounded Little Me. I will also be right by your side as we move into the heart of the work. You are not alone.

CHAPTER 5

Healing Little Me from the Inside Out

As you now know, the relationship you have with your Little Me influences how your relationships with others play out, especially your intimate ones. The core wounds your Little Me sustained in childhood guide the kinds of relationships you instinctively seek out as an adult because the part of you that learned a particularly painful way to love and be loved never got the nurturing needed to grow up. In the last chapter, you met the nurturing parts of you that can be called on to help soothe your wounded Little Me any time they are upset. Even better, over time these Inner Nurturers can help create a safe and supportive environment that can make room for—and contain—your deepest feelings. Just like an attentive, responsible, and loving parent, these wise parts of you allow freedom of emotional expression while creating boundaries that keep you safe. Offering the kind of unconditional support that so many of us did not receive in childhood, they always have our back.

Inviting these parts to take the lead as you learn how to access the steady, kind, nurturing energy that can always help Little Me is essential to the work of becoming self-full. To begin this process, we're going to spend some more time learning how to work with your Inner Nurturers to help heal your wounded Little Me. This is also the kind of work you can do with a healer, a therapist, or a coach—and I highly recommend finding extra professional support to help you on your path to becoming self-full. I can also be that kind of presence for you through this book. The beauty of leaning on these loving people is that you are building your own internal healing community. Once you have a strong community of Inner Nurturers on speed dial, you will never have to depend solely on others outside yourself for the love and support you need.

They provide the safety to get to know aspects of your Little Me as if they were your own children. It means learning to notice the signs that these aspects are being awakened or feel like acting out. Your Inner Nurturers can sit with them and listen to what they need. It means becoming so attuned to their emotional state that you are able to help them name what they are feeling at any given time and to understand that their emotional turmoil is temporary. Essentially, it means becoming their rock, so that when their fear of abandonment seems overwhelming, they will no longer cling to whatever or whomever they can in a desperate attempt to feel safe because they know they have a rich community of support right inside their own heart.

Some people refer to this process as *re-parenting*, as it is essentially the work of receiving what your primary caregivers could not provide enough of when you were a child. As this community of care strengthens, a kind of internal co-regulation blossoms. Throughout our lives, we need and want to find close connection with others. It's part of who we are as human beings. Healing your wounded Little Me will make this a joyful process of growth rather than a desperate search for somebody else to complete you. As you heal, you will see that simultaneously you start to lean on many healthy supportive people both with your Inner Nurturers and with the people who you trust to help you while you reach out to people who have this warm, supportive quality to them in your current world.

It's important that you take your time and go at your own pace as we begin this work together. There's no goal to be reached, and no gold star for getting it right. Your Little Me parts will always be with you, and they will always need comforting and tending. Learning to put your trust in your Inner Nurturers as well as others accompanying you on this journey is an ongoing process, something that may feel unfamiliar at first but will give you a steadily growing sense of inner security.

LEARNING TO BE WITH LITTLE ME

The first step toward getting to know your Little Me parts is to cultivate an awareness of how you are currently relating to them. We touched on this in the last chapter, when we noticed how the voice of your Inner Protectors often hurts them while also seeking to protect them. Now let's go a little deeper and actually sit down with whatever aspect of your Little Me is closest to see what they have to say.

This might not come naturally at first, which is completely normal and very much okay. The truth is, we live in a society where feelings are often perceived as messy or uncomfortable, not to mention far too time-consuming. The majority of us grew up in homes where *emotional bypassing* was the norm, and where our parents—no matter how loving—were too busy or distracted to sit with us and take the time to hear what we were feeling. Instead, if we were upset, we may have gotten a hug or an "it'll be okay," or been given a cookie or some extra time in front of the TV. Not that anybody is to blame in this scenario. It's only recently that conversations about mental health and *emotional intelligence* are becoming more mainstream. Chances are, our parents didn't know how to sit with their own feelings, either. Faced with difficult emotions, the common response is to try to fix them as quickly as possible—whether this means medicating them away (with alcohol or prescription drugs) or simply putting on a brave face and pretending that everything is okay.

As kids, this means we learn to do the same because that's what's required of us to be part of the family. What we really need is parents who model what it means to hold space for the full spectrum of our emotional experience. The proud, joyful, excited feelings, *and* the difficult, painful, and confusing ones. If you consider how uncomfortable it makes most of us to see another person in distress, and how quickly we turn to whatever is on hand to distract us from anything that feels bad (be it food, work, shopping, drugs, scrolling through social media, working out, you name it), it is clear that when it comes to being with our feelings, society has a long way to go.

When we are so quick to bypass painful emotions, this leaves no room to learn how to move *through* the emotions we are experiencing in a healthy and supported way. It also means we have forgotten the magic and the medicine that can be found *within* the pain and the messiness of it all; that the catalyst to healing lies in being brave enough to feel and hold space for the wounded parts of us that are desperate to be seen and heard. These are the parts that have likely never had their needs met, that have information that is vital for our overall well-being, and that are often simply craving the attention of somebody who cares. All our feelings need to know they matter, all our feelings need to be heard, and all our feelings have a right to be acknowledged. When it comes to healing your wounded Little Me, this is where your Inner Nurturers come in and start to validate all of you.

The only way you can be the wise advocate for all aspects of your Little Me is to learn to listen to everything they have to say, which first means learning to sit with them in as much stillness as you can manage on any given day, something that is not easy for anybody who is anxiously attached. As discussed, we have often learned to be hypervigilant to the outside world as a way to stay safe, carefully monitoring the actions and reactions of others for clues that we may be abandoned and (in the case of a very young child who relied on their caregivers for survival) literally left to die. While this helps us develop a sensitivity to the needs of others, it is also part of how we maintained a sense of stability. But it has also come at a cost, as we have become more attuned with what's going on around us than what's happening inside us.

The busier and more distracted we are, and the more we continue to look for love outside of ourselves, the harder it will be to hear Little Me, let alone to call on the love and support of our Inner Nurturers. As we open to this supportive community, we will be developing *internal empathy* for our wounded Little Me. Slowing down also means being present with our pain—and as we have discussed, as a society we don't know how to be with hurt. So let's take it slowly, together.

♥♥

WHERE IT HURTS
IS WHERE THE HEALING IS

No matter how well-adjusted our lives or how fortunate we are, all humans experience pain. In the case of Little Me, the core wounds we carry are often as old as we are, to the extent they even seem like they are part of us. When we are unable to process this old pain, it becomes trapped inside of our bodies, coloring our entire experience of the world and preventing us from living a full and satisfying life.

While we naturally prefer not to experience pain, with caring support we can learn to be fully present for what's inside our hearts, which includes the pain of not feeling loved or not having our needs met. When we put up the necessary barriers to protect ourselves from these angry, hurting parts, we also create blocks to the joy that is also always available to us in our heart space. Because of this, instead of tapping into our natural source of happiness and well-being, we must chase after external pleasures to make us feel better. As I described in chapter 3, chasing after another person as either a balm for our wounds or a distraction from being with our pain is what leads to codependency and love addiction.

Now, we're going to commit to feeling and experiencing the messages this body is sending you. This is what I call *leaning into* your feelings. It's important to remember that *all your feelings are okay*. What I mean by this is that there is no such thing as a "good" or a "bad" feeling. We often hear people talk about positive and negative feelings, but really all feelings are important communication about what is happening inside us right now. The labels of "good" and "bad" often mean that parents or caregivers struggle to know how to validate our emotional experience by witnessing and honoring whatever it is we are feeling, no matter how painful, confusing, or inconvenient.

For example, as a child you might have felt upset about not being picked up from school. Perhaps your parents had a flat tire or something else came up that caused them to be late, while you went into panic mode. By the time they arrived, you might have been visibly distressed, causing them to ask you, "Why are you so upset? I'm here now. You have no reason to be scared!" This seems like a natural response, right? They want to let you know you're safe. But it's actually an example of emotional bypassing—and in the moment, it suggests that your feelings of distress are either not real or wrong. You may be able to sense in your own body right now how it feels to have your feelings criticized or denied.

A parent who is able to validate your feelings, on the other hand, thus letting you know that your needs are being recognized and understood, might instead ask you to share how you feel about them being late. After listening closely to what you have to say, they may nod and tell you, "Yes, it makes sense that you were worried. It must have been scary not knowing where I was." Take a minute to sense how that feels in your body.

Ultimately, parents feel bad when they let their kids down. They can get defensive if they indirectly caused pain and try to gloss over their own shortcomings, partly to make themselves feel better. Guilt is another negative emotion, after all, and nobody wants to feel like they are a bad parent. Easier to pretend to themselves and to you that whatever happened and whatever feelings it gave rise to aren't a big deal (especially in an example like the one above, where nobody got physically hurt). But, over time, the bypassing of these emotional experiences leaves us feeling confused and vulnerable. As we know, the small child who didn't get their needs met never grows up; they live on as your wounded Little Me.

This is not about blaming anyone. We all often bypass our feelings because it's what we've learned to do. But ultimately our feelings are the messengers of our emotional needs. When we fail to validate what we are feeling, we are not giving ourselves permission to feel the way we do, which in turn means we are also not permitted to need what we do. Making room for these feelings means learning how to receive the gift of validation from your Inner Nurturers and those accompanying you on this journey. It is a vital step in learning how to meet your emotional needs on an ongoing basis, either with the help of your inner community or by asking for them to be met in a healthy way by those who can show up for you.

You can practice inner validation by simply thinking of something that makes you feel upset. Notice and name the emotion, perhaps tracking what it feels like in your body. Then listen for what your Inner Nurturers might say to you. Over the course of this book, I'm becoming one of them, so you could even imagine that I might say, "It's good to feel what you feel. We can be curious together about what it means." You can stop right there if you notice that your body relaxes as you feel heard. If you get the sense that this feeling is bigger than the current situation seems to warrant, you might ask when you have felt like this before. There is not always a quick answer to this question, but your inner world appreciates you slowing down to make the inquiry. If you do get a sense of how the current emotion is connected to the past, it can begin to make sense that you would feel upset by this now as well. You are simply noticing the *emotional logic* behind what you are feeling, in the same way as the parent who was late.

It is also helpful to have an Inner Safe Place where your community of Inner Nurturers can sit with all aspects of your Little Me anytime and tend to what is coming up for them. They can communicate through inner dialogue (inner hearing), and you may also visualize them meeting with your mind's eye (inner seeing). I can see my kind grandmother and hear her voice when my Little Me needs to be heard. Your capacity for inner feeling will allow any emotions that need to be felt to be present.

For the following exercise, we're going to create a place for them to meet using your inner seeing, which will require you to visualize this experience. To help you remember what your Little Me looks like, find a photo of your younger self that you feel a connection to and have it close by during this exercise. We can do this exercise together with the extended audio version at **beselffull.com /meditations**. If at any time you start to feel upset or that the experience is moving too quickly, you can stop, open your eyes, push your feet into the ground, and feel the presence of someone you trust. This is listening to the voice of Little Me as well.

The Inner Safe Place

1. Start by lying down in a comfortable position and, if possible, bring something to cover your eyes and block the light. Close your eyes and take some deep breaths into your heart space. Drop your exhales to pour around your heart while extending your breathing. Practice this for ten to fifteen breaths. Feel your nervous system get more relaxed. Learning how to slow down your breathing and feel into your heart might be challenging at first, so only do as many breaths as feel comfortable. Breathing this way may even bring up memories, so be gentle with yourself if that happens.

2. Now think of a "Safe Place." Maybe it's a place from your past where you always felt safe. Or it might be a place in nature. Remember the details of how it looks, feels, and smells. For example, if it's a beach, you may feel a breeze on your face and the sand below your feet. As you envision this Safe Place, notice how calm you feel here.

3. Now invite the aspects of your Little Me to come. Picture them and see them in their Safe Place, noticing how they are sitting or standing. If you're struggling to get them to show up, this just means they need some more time to trust that

it's safe. Just keep the invitation open for them, and try the rest of the exercise another day. (I'll share more below about why they may be shy.)

4. Once you can see your Little Me, invite your Inner Nurturers to join them in their Safe Place, noticing which of your community of care arrives. Invite them to introduce themselves. For example: "Hello, Little Me. I am here to see you, to hear you, and to help you. Whatever you need, I am here." Have them explain to Little Me that they can handle whatever Little Me has to say and that Little Me has complete permission to show up and express all of themselves.

5. Now invite your Inner Nurturers to ask Little Me what they are feeling, and see if Little Me is able to share in this moment. Then listen deeply using your inner hearing and simply validate whatever is shared. There's a good chance some parts of Little Me feel lonely or empty, sad or angry. Remember, the Inner Nurturer does not need to try to fix them. Simply let these parts of Little Me know that the way they are feeling is welcome here. Tell them they are allowed to feel all those things and that you are here for them.

6. When they have said everything that they need to, tell these aspects of Little Me that you are always here to listen to them and give them love. Let them know that you will be checking in regularly, and that the more they share, the better you will be able to understand what they need.

7. Before you close, ask Little Me to stay in your heart center so that you can hold them in the most sacred part of your body. You can even visualize making these little ones very small and moving them from their Safe Place into your heart. If you have it close by, you can hold the photo close to your heart space, inviting them in for safekeeping.

8. Slowly open your eyes and ground yourself back into the room. Take some big inhales and exhales, just noticing where you are and what's in the room.

All aspects of Little Me need to feel seen and heard, but it may take a while for them to trust your Inner Nurturers. They may have been ignored for so long that it is hard to imagine anyone will listen. Please don't get discouraged if they didn't show up at first, or if they weren't able to share what they're feeling. Remember, others have let Little Me down, and you might have to repeat this exercise a few times before they feel safe to dialogue with you. But now you will always have this Safe Place inside to go to, and returning here often will show your Little Me parts that you are committed to being there for them, to understanding their needs, and to hearing what they have to say. Inviting your Inner Nurturers to witness and validate the feelings of your wounded Little Me means giving yourself permission to feel whatever comes up, without any stories about why they "should" or "shouldn't" feel that way. This will remind your Little Me that none of their feelings are wrong, that it is okay to feel it all, and that there is a resource deep inside of you where they can always turn to get the support they need.

This means that as you dive deeper into this work, you will also have to be committed enough to keep turning down volume on the outside (not devoting all your attention to your relationship and not actively pursuing distractions), so you can pay more attention to your inner experience. As you learn to navigate through life using this inner compass, you will gradually build more trust in your own ability to rely on the community of Nurturers inside, and you will be less likely to hand over the entire responsibility for this to somebody else.

REAL SELF-LOVE

As a culture, we are becoming very familiar with the concept of *self-love*, but we often bypass the fact that *real* self-love is actually the hard work of showing up for *all* of our selves. Taking some time for a trip to the spa or into nature may help you connect to your inner world, an essential first step in learning to be with Little Me. But it can't stop there. As messy and scary as it may feel, making a commitment to being present with all the feelings that come up when you linger a little longer is vital.

As you begin to touch these deeper feelings, you may find you are pulled toward the protections you have learned to ease the pain. These might be cookies, Netflix binges, a glass of wine, scrolling through social media, or some internet shopping. When these urges arise, it might be your inner world signaling the need to slow down and take a short break from doing the inner work. If you do find yourself going toward a particular favorite diversion, you could ask, "What would I have to feel if I didn't eat this cookie?" Offering to hear your inner world in this way is such an honoring and respectful thing to do. If after pausing and listening, you still feel pulled toward the cookie, you won't be doing anything wrong by having it. One of the best ways to ease your way into this work is with the company of supportive friends. Reaching out in this way may help you need other kinds of soothing less. Always remember, you can go as slowly as you like.

As for what may come up, some of the hardest feelings, and the most repressed in those who are anxiously attached, are anger, sadness, and shame. In fact, even reading these words may make you aware of the heaviness in your heart. It is especially important to learn to lean into these feelings in particular. Anger can be the scariest. Our anger wants to protect us and to see justice done by way of an apology or other form of reparations. And while a healthy expression of anger might mean you let a person know exactly how they have hurt you, even the thought of a conversation like this can wake up a core abandonment wound when it threatens your attachment to a partner. What if your partner's response is to get defensive and shut you out completely? Is it worth the risk to ask for what you need?

Easier to act like things are fine and simply stick another Band-Aid on the part of you that hurts, adding yet more weight to your heavy, heavy heart. But, over time, this heaviness then manifests as grief for the part of you that is literally *dying* to be heard deep down inside. When that grief is ignored, we can sink toward depression.

As your Inner Nurturers begin to attune to the needs of your

Little Me, notice when this anger and sadness surface during your days. Then invite Little Me into your Safe Place, and allow them to get mad, to grieve, and maybe even to sob. Your Inner Nurturers can help Little Me feel validated and seen. Allow this process to be gentle and ongoing. You aren't going to heal in one sitting. Instead, see this as part of the ongoing work of becoming self-full and just another element to living a joyous, whole, and self-full life.

SAY WHAT YOU FEEL

No one wakes up in the morning, stretches, and thinks, "What a beautiful day! It's the perfect morning to sit and have a chat with my inner pain!" Usually, we avoid this process for as long as humanly possible. To make it easier, it can help to name what's coming up as you learn to lean into your feelings—as this allows you to become the observer of your emotions versus feeling like they are all of you. Being the observer allows you to have enough space to watch the emotions and let them move through you without getting overwhelmed by them. The more healing you do, the greater your capacity for being the observer. And the more you are able to observe, the more open you are to healing, so practicing this creates a beautiful circle that supports becoming self-full.

Any time your wounded Little Me parts are asking for your attention, label their feelings as they come up: "I feel fearful," "I feel worried," "I feel furious," "I feel let down." Say it out loud if you like. This way, when a strong emotion arises, the feeling can be seen for what it is, and from this zoomed-out perspective, it also becomes easier to see what needs to be tended to. In the initial stages of connecting with your feelings, you may sometimes feel swept away by them. That's okay and to be expected. You can simply begin again with the next wave of feeling.

Interpersonal neurobiologist Dan Siegel also shares how labeling your feelings helps connect the logical side of the brain to the emotional side in his book *Mindsight*. "Naming an affect (an observable sign of emotion) soothes limbic firing. Sometimes we need to 'name it to tame it.'" What he's referring to is the fact that our emotional reactions to our experiences are stored in the limbic system of the brain, specifically the amygdala. In the case of painful or frightening experiences, these become our core wounds, and they may be reactivated anytime we encounter a reminder of the original event. Going against all logic, it is as if we are transported back in time to when this experience overwhelmed our system (often in our childhood). Without help, wounded Little Me will be pulled into acting from this place.

By simply naming or labeling what you are feeling in the moment, you bring the logical, thinking prefrontal cortex online to mediate. You are also acknowledging and reflecting to Little Me that you see and understand their experience. This combination of reason and kindness is very powerful. Once you have given your emotional reaction a name, you are able to ask, "Is this an appropriate response?" The answer is actually complicated. From the perspective of Little Me's earlier experience, it *is* appropriate, even when the reaction looks bigger than the current event. Most important, this arrival of big feelings is an invitation to sit with Little

Me's initial experience, so you can validate and heal it. This is when your Inner Nurturer can invite your Little Me into your Safe Place, to see if they will tell you how old you were when you first experienced this pain. Notice if naming feelings for your Little Me parts makes it feel safer for them to share more clues about the core wound that sits underneath.

BECOMING AWARE OF YOUR ANS RESPONSES

As we know, when we feel frightened in our relationships, childhood trauma reawakens. This fear appropriately shifts us into the primal reaction mode we learned about in chapter 1, where the nervous system creates such powerful physical responses to a perceived threat that you have no option but to act on them. Remember how the ANS (which is in charge of monitoring the safety of our connections) connects our physical organs to our brain? When we're activated in this way, our logical thinking shuts down so we can respond more quickly. We slide down the evolutionary ladder from our safe ventral state (where we are wired for connection) into our sympathetic state, which tells us to fight or flee, or our dorsal state, which tells us we need to shut down completely until it is safe to reconnect. And this can happen so fast. For example, if your partner doesn't text back for a while, you may suddenly feel the pain and fear of being forgotten and be swept away by your sympathetic system. Under these circumstances, you can't always call on your Inner

Nurturer, as your body is putting all of its energy and focus into protection and survival. But as you heal, you will be able to remain aware of the fact that your ANS has been touched by something powerful in either your inner or outer world.

With awareness and compassion for this process, you can remind yourself that any sympathetic response that might have made sense *then* is now an opportunity to be with the Little Me who is holding this trauma. Over time, simply noticing "this may be old wiring" when you feel a sympathetic activation happening can begin to slow the process. And then there is the opportunity to bring your Nurturers in to sit with whatever hurt or scared this Little Me. You will discover that the greater the healing, the greater the neuroception of safety *on the inside*, the easier it will be to return to the ventral state. The below exercise shows you one way to nurture your ANS.

SANCTUARY FOR A FRIGHTENED ANS

In our most intimate relationships, when something happens that stirs up our feelings of possible abandonment, we may feel our bodies begin to react. Reminded of our childhood core wound, we no longer feel safe, so our sympathetic nervous system comes online. When our ANS is really activated the best course of action is to focus on another system we have control of in the heat of the moment. That is your respiratory system. Breathing in the way outlined below allows for a temporary return to feelings of safety. Think of it like respite care for your ANS while you do the hard inner work of changing your inner landscape and making ventral your base-line state.

1. Notice how you feel in your body and name what is happening (for example: "My breathing is becoming shallow, I feel tight in my chest, my stomach feels queasy").

2. Say out loud to yourself: "This is old wiring and firing." Notice that your radar has detected danger and your sympathetic nervous system is coming online.

3. Breathe in so that your stomach expands, and work on extending your exhales so that they are longer than your inhales. Your stomach will expand as it fills with air, the opposite way than you're probably used to. For example, breathe in for a count of four and out for a count of five or six. Release the breath through the crown of your head. Notice how this starts to slow things down. Breathing this way helps your body signal to your brain that you are okay. Feel your breath and bring your breath into your belly. Focus on following the feeling rather than a thought.

4. If you have to think and you can't just feel, then repeat the words *inhale* and *exhale*, while you go back to focusing on the feeling of breath filling your belly and leaving.

5. Tell yourself that the reaction you are having in this moment is *old firing*. Tell yourself: "I will be okay no matter what."

6. If you can't go somewhere private and safe, now you can go to your Inner Safe Place and call on your Inner Nurturer to help. You may or may not be able to reach this step, but the more you practice steps one through five, the more quickly you will become calm enough to connect.

7. Whenever possible, call on a supportive friend who you know to be consistent and reliable, and ask if they have a moment to hold some empathetic space for you. Connecting with another trustworthy nervous system always increases safety.

Before you begin the above, ground yourself by placing both feet flat on the floor and visualize the earth beneath, bringing to mind the image of somebody you trust. These simple additional steps will help calm you down, in and of themselves, if this breathing exercise feels like it might be too much.

Once your ANS has cooled down, your perception may have shifted enough so that you are experiencing from a more here-and-now sense of things rather than being overwhelmed by this past experience. Over time, and with practice, you will begin to strengthen your ventral system so that you can slow down and attend to the experience your Little Me is having. In the meantime, please be gentle with yourself. The feelings that come up when we're in this heightened state can be scary, and I know from personal experience how hard it is to not react to them. Anger may flare up, or you may want to run away or simply feel like collapsing. Perhaps you even find yourself issuing a desperate ultimatum to your partner: "If you continue like this I'm leaving and never coming back!"

But these extreme reactions will only cause more conflict—both in your external relationships and within yourself. Breathing deep into your diaphragm actually sends a little message to your brain that you are okay. With practice, you'll be able to shift back into a state of calmness that allows for connection to be re-established with yourself and sometimes with your partner. We'll be looking more closely at how to communicate with your upset Little Me during heated situations in chapter 8. But first, let's see what happens when we learn how to welcome and accept the parts of you that get so fired up in the first place.

ADOPTING YOUR FULL SELF AND GIVING HER WHAT SHE NEEDS

The work of healing your wounded Little Me means showing them that you love and accept *all* aspects of them, no matter what. I like to think of this as literally adopting the parts you learned to squash down or hide away in order to stay connected to those who couldn't fully embrace all of you. When it comes to healing the core abandonment wound that so often leads to a person becoming anxiously attached, adopting these parts can be extremely powerful when cultivating healthy relationships with yourself and others.

How did these parts get pushed away in the first place? Maybe you got made fun of at school for the way you looked or something you said, causing you to shut down parts of yourself that you learned were "not okay." Maybe your parents feared conflict, so they couldn't welcome your sad or angry or jealous parts. These parts become wounded as a result and get buried deep, deep inside. The truth is, we all possess what are labeled "positive" and "negative" qualities. The positive ones are those that our families valued, and the negative ones are either the unwanted wounded parts or the Protectors we developed to shelter us from the pain of Little Me's core wounds. If you have "greedy" or "bossy" parts, for example, they are trying to get something for you to comfort the pain of not getting what you really needed. One of my clients had a strongly controlling part because she had to try to organize the chaos of a household with two alcoholic parents. Because the abandonment wound had no opportunity to heal, any time she tried to be less controlling, she felt the terror of the drunken chaos well up, so she would immediately call on her controlling Protector to stop the fear from overwhelming her.

The Inner Protectors need to stay in place until the Little Me parts that experienced the pain and fear are seen, validated, and also receive what they needed at the time but didn't get. A big part of this is just being warmly witnessed and understood, but it is also important that there is safety if there has been fear, acceptance if there has been shame, comfort if there has been pain, and togetherness if there has been abandonment. These are called *reparative* or *disconfirming experiences*, and literally change the felt sense of the implicit memories that hold Little Me's traumas.

Once the pain is relieved, the Inner Protectors don't need to desperately cling to their way of being in order to keep the pain and fear at bay. As my controlling client's Little Me brought her terror into our time together, she found a Safe Place in the quiet of my office and shelter in my calm ventral nervous system. Being in this quiet, session after session, bathed her in what she had needed at the time—understanding, warmth, and safety. And her need to control also let go bit by bit, much to everyone's relief.

Exercise: Steps to Adopt Your Full Selves and Give Them What They Need

As humans, we are all born with the potential to love everything and everyone equally and unconditionally. Ideally, we are also able to trust that everyone loves *us* equally and unconditionally. But of course, life experience teaches us that this is not the case. Now let's connect with your Little Me again to seek clues from your past about the parts of you that learned they were unworthy or unlovable, so that you and your Inner Nurturers can begin to give you the unconditional love you deserve. Keep a journal and pen next to you for this adoption and healing exercise. While I am going to offer all the steps in the exercise here, you can do it in small increments. We're going to be using photos to anchor this practice. You can move through them at your own pace, perhaps one photo at a time. You may even find that you stay with a single photo for several sessions of doing this exercise. Just be guided by what you sense is the best pace for you.

1. Hunt down between five and ten photos of yourself from different points in your childhood to work with. Maybe

make a trip to your mom's house to borrow her old photo albums or ask a relative to text some pics. Print them out if needed.

2. Invite your Inner Nurturers to be with you as you begin. With the photos in hand, take ten comfortably deep breaths into your heart center, feeling your chest expand. Extend your breath, but not to the point that you become light-headed. As you breathe, visualize air entering your mouth or nose and traveling down into your heart.

3. Choose a photo to look at while continuing to breathe deeply into your heart. Bring this child into your heart center.

4. Write down all the feelings that come up for you now, in the present moment. Examples include "This photo of me and my brother at summer camp makes me feel excited and free," or "This photo of me at an amusement park makes me pissed off with my dad."

5. Acknowledge and write down any memories, desires, or thoughts that surface with each feeling. "I wish I still kept in touch with my brother. Why have we drifted apart?" or "I hated the scary rides, but Dad pushed me to go on them."

6. Close your eyes and transport yourself back to the time the photo was taken, to the best of your ability. Try to identify your age and invite the feelings from that time into your

body. See what other stories from that time might come, too. Journal about what you recall.

7. Invite the deeper feelings you had as a child to arise in your mind. Write them down, too. For example: "Underneath that smile, I was really unhappy. I didn't want to be there." Are there any thoughts that are associated with these feelings?

8. With the support of your Inner Nurturers, ask, "What was I not getting back then that I needed?" For example, maybe you craved more attention from your parents or perhaps you wanted to play more than you were allowed to.

9. Repeat this process with each of your photos. Once you have written down your feelings, thoughts, and unmet needs for all of them, reread everything. Can you notice which parts of yourself you learned were not "okay"?

10. As you gather these moments, feelings, and snapshots, start to notice if you are judging or pushing parts of yourself away. This may be an undesired personality trait, a story about how you were ugly or not smart, or underlying feelings of shame.

11. The final step is to begin to look at your Little Me parts with loving new eyes. Eyes that do not judge them and that accept all that they are. Your Inner Nurturers are very good at sensing what these young ones needed at the time but didn't get.

These parts of our selves can surround each aspect of Little Me with the comfort or safety or acceptance that was missing. As this repair of what was wounded is complete, these Little Me parts will feel more settled and freer from the pain and fear they have lived in since the trauma happened. Let them know how much you love them and that everything they have experienced is an important part of their story.

When I did this exercise for the first time, I did *not* recall happy times—only pain and shame. I was chunky in my teens, and I found that I wanted to look away from photos of me then much more than I wanted to look at them. It was clear that I couldn't fully accept this chubby adolescent. Compared to other girls my age, I was also short, and I was the last to get my period. My feelings and thoughts from that time made it clear that I had core wounds that led me to believe: *I am not lovable* and *There is something wrong with me.*

Over time, I had shoved this little girl and her painful feelings of being "less than" away, but of course they were always there under the surface all along, forming the foundation of the Little Me Pact I made over and over in my painful adult relationships. Connecting to the late bloomer in this photograph, I could literally see at what point self-love had become conditional, eventually morphing into self-loathing. I was then able to ask my Inner Nurturers to let her know that her feelings of shame and loneliness were entirely understandable, and that this girl would always be accepted as a part of me, no matter what. Over time, the shame melted in the light of acceptance and understanding, and that made room for her to be welcomed as much as any other part.

Once you have chosen to unconditionally accept your wounded Little Me parts, and you begin to listen to all they have to say, you will become more practiced at communicating with them. As you catch yourself flying off the handle at something, or stuffing down your feelings about a situation, you will be more likely to pause and consider why you might be reacting this way, asking yourself: "What's really going on here? What am I really reacting to—the situation or an old wound? Why do I feel ashamed about the way I feel?"—all questions that will open the dialogue between your wounded Little Me and your Inner Nurturers.

FOR THE LOVE OF GIGI

Now let's take a look at how learning to validate and accept all of your feelings and healing the old wounds by receiving what was needed at the time but was not available then can help you become strong enough to turn to your own inner resources when things feel upset in your love life. Remember, sharing your process with a trusted person at times is another way of adding to these inner resources by internalizing the necessary experience of being received by another exactly as you are.

My client Stacy first came to me when she was grieving the loss of her dog, Gigi, a fifteen-year-old rescue. As we worked through her feelings of loss, it became clear that some deeper issues in her partnership were being activated anytime she tried to express her sadness about this loss to her partner, Olivia. Stacy shared that she didn't have a whole lot of complaints about Olivia, mostly experiencing a rock-solid relationship where they also enjoyed each other's company, but when Gigi passed away, they hit a major speed bump.

What began to happen was that Stacy would turn to Olivia for support in processing her loss. But every time Stacy would bring up her pain, Olivia would quickly respond with invalidating comments, such as: "Don't be sad" or "At least you had fifteen good years together." At times Olivia would avoid Stacy altogether when she sensed her getting sad. This awakened feelings in Stacy around not being seen and held in the intense pain she was experiencing, and she shared that she had begun to feel that Olivia didn't care about what she was going through, which left her feeling abandoned.

During our sessions, on the other hand, I simply held space for her to feel her pain. I often shared validating statements the same way an Inner Nurturer would, such as: "Of course it hurts. Losing Gigi has been like losing a best friend" or "It's perfectly normal to have times when you feel sadness—and this is really sad." I could see that Stacy didn't have a Safe Place (external or internal) to feel her pain, and she hadn't had enough external validation in her early life to be able to do this within herself. Our time together was going to provide the yeast that would let this capacity grow in her. Her partner, Olivia, wasn't intentionally trying to hurt Stacy—in fact, she was trying to make her feel better—but the more ignored Stacy felt by Olivia's invalidating comments, the more irritable and angry she became with her partner.

Stacy and Olivia were able to work through these issues when Stacy also learned why it was hard for Olivia to show up. She was uncomfortable with Stacy's pain for reasons of her own that were completely unrelated to the love she felt for Stacy. But the real magic happened for Stacy when she learned to connect to her own Inner Nurturer, in the form of her warm grandmother, to help hold her pain. Her whole body remembered sitting on her grandma's lap anytime she felt sad about any little thing, much less the big things. She could relax into her tears then, knowing they were being heard.

Gigi's passing ended up also being a beautiful catalyst for Stacy to grieve some other times in her life when she felt loss and abandonment but had not had the support to be with it all. Feelings of abandonment often accumulate over time. If we aren't able to process them as we go, the pain builds up until a single event tips the balance, awakening a flood of old feelings—and causing us to lash out at whomever we happen to have made responsible for our feelings. In the case of a romantic relationship, this is just part of our Little Me Pact.

Stacy's story shows how balance is restored in our bodies and our relationships as we allow ourselves to feel and be with the full range of our emotions. This happens when we allow them to surface and be met with what they needed at the time but wasn't available from the people around us the first time we experienced them. For example, an anxious mother may have trouble listening to and soothing a sad child because she is already so upset herself. No one is to blame, and yet the wound of being abandoned in her moment of distress is real for this young person. To heal, the pain needs to be expressed again and lovingly received this time. If we have enough inner resources, we may be able to do this on our own. If we don't yet have these internalized others to help us, then expressing the pain to someone we trust to listen and hold us will be a balm for the wound and, in the process, this person's presence and comfort will become an inner resource for another day. The pain stored in our heart space can only be released by being felt, or it will remain stagnant and stuck, infecting us like a poison and blocking our capacity to give and receive love. Since releasing pain around abandonment in this way and being fully received in the reality and truth of these feelings is core to becoming self-full, we'll be doing more work around this in the next chapter.

YOU ARE *SO* WORTH IT

As you are beginning to have the experience of finding a home for all your feelings and tenderly caring for all aspects of your Little Me, you are likely starting to sense that this is what makes you a perfectly imperfect, whole human being. By strengthening your internal resources and adopting the parts that got disowned, you are able to know yourself with all your strengths and all your challenges. Gradually, this will also help you understand that you are inherently worthy of unconditional love. One beautiful gift of doing this is that you will also be able to receive your partner and others with whom you're close as whole human beings as well. It is the secure foundation for relationships that last.

Most of us who are anxiously attached struggle with feelings of low self-worth. It is another by-product of having to reject or disown parts of our selves in order to belong in our family. When we haven't received the validation we need, we tend to live in a world where we consistently feel like there is something wrong with us. As we are learning to bring in our Inner Nurturers to help with abandonment, we are also providing the aspects of Little Me that feel not good enough to deserve love or attention with the acceptance they have needed all along. This inner consolation is what we really crave, although our consumer culture teaches us otherwise. It offers a gazillion ways for us to feel better on the outside, but the truth is that no achievement or possession will bring us a lasting sense of self-worth: no six-figure salary, no designer gadgets, no size-two butt.

The other struggle for us comes in the form of the popular message that being loved by another is what determines our worth—something many of us have found resonates with our core wound. Our Little Me can't help but believe, *Well, if this partner loves me, then I must be worthy of love.* After all, this is what we have been waiting for since childhood: someone to love us so we see our worth reflected in their eyes. Rather than risk finding out that this partner can't love us, we overextend, ignore our own needs, and squash down our anger because it might push our partner away. In other words, we become selfless to protect ourselves from feeling once again that we are unworthy of love. Between what our culture has taught us and what we have experienced as children, our Inner Protectors push and push: "You must try harder, do more, lose more weight to prove to them that you are worthy." But the truth is that real self-worth comes from within, and from an inner knowing that you have nothing to prove, and that you are always worthy of love. Doing this work is when we discover that we are neither "less than" or "better than" anybody else—that we are, in fact, "just right" as we are. With practice, working with your Inner Nurturers in the way outlined in this chapter will slowly become your norm, and the critical voices of your Inner Protectors will be needed less.

Beginning to feel that this is where we're headed can be inspiration for the sometimes painful work of becoming self-full that I will continue to guide you through in the coming pages. In this chapter, you have learned how to be brave and lean into your feelings and how to invite your community of Inner Nurturers to validate and adopt all the different parts of your wounded Little Me. I want you to continue to connect to these parts of yourself as you move through this work. Throughout the day, ask your Inner Nurturers to let your Little Me know: "You are not alone" and "You are enough just as you are." If they can't quite take it in yet, just listen to what Little Me does want to share with you. Next, we'll expand and deepen this process on our way to moving from selfless to self-full.

CHAPTER 6

From Selfless to Self-Full

How does it feel to meet your community of Inner Nurturers and have them sit with you and actually ask you how you feel? To realize that these loving, supportive parts of yourself are always there for you, no matter what? Maybe it seems hard to believe. Perhaps it brings up feelings of vulnerability and lack of trust. Or maybe you are already beginning to get a sense of how empowering it is to know that you have inner resources that you can always turn to for reassurance that you're okay. You are on the road to gaining a deep, intrinsic knowing that so much of what you need is available to you on the inside, right here and right now.

It takes time and commitment to unravel the experiences that led to you becoming anxiously attached, and heal your core wounds so you can make secure attachments based on mutual reciprocity with a partner. The process we began in the previous chapter is a core component of moving from selfless to self-full; that is, from feeling completely dependent on others for love and support to arriving in a relationship with your own strong inner resources intact.

We've touched on what it means to be "selfless" at various points during this book. Let's do a quick review. Through early life experiences, we have come to believe that we are being overly demanding if we have needs of our own. When we expressed these reasonable wishes, this was often met with what felt like disapproval or rejection by those closest to us, and so we came to understand, in the deepest way, that we will be met with more of the same if we express our needs to a partner. This means that as adults, we do our best to put our partners' needs first, while ignoring our own. Because our needs were not allowed, our wounded Little Me believes that we are not inherently worthy of love, and so it must be earned by overextending ourselves in our relationships. We have come to believe that acts of selflessness must be what make us a "good person." After all, nobody wants to be seen as selfish. But remember, there's a big difference between being selfish and becoming self-full. In this chapter, we will continue the work of filling ourselves up with inner love and support while we continue to support our Little Me parts in their healing. Through this work, you will be able to give to others from a cup that feels full.

First, let's take a closer look at what it means to be selfless, how we got to be this way, and why it is deeply interwoven with being anxiously attached.

♥♥

INNER ABANDONMENT
AND THE RESCUE FANTASY

At its core, selflessness stems from a deeply felt sense of inner abandonment. With no intention to cause us pain, our parents probably didn't have the inner resources to attend to us in a way that we felt our needs or desires mattered. We internalize everyone with whom we have an emotionally meaningful relationship, so we took these absent parents into our inner world where they continue to reflect the unimportance of our needs long after we leave home. Before too long, we simply lose track of having needs or desires that matter because we are so focused on being how we have to be for our parents to stay connected with us.

We will do whatever we have to do to get the connection we need. The price of being a member of the family is sometimes very high and very painful. For example, if my parents are not self-full because of their own upbringings, the best they are able to offer is inconsistent love and attention. We adapt by learning which of our behaviors keeps them close as often as possible, pushing the parts of us that need something far away. One child learns that sadness shuts down her mother, so her sorrowful self goes underground, unattended. Another child finds that her aliveness, her joy, is intolerable to her parents, so she grows quiet and depressed. Two things are happening: We are dividing our selves up into acceptable and unacceptable parts, and we are spending almost all our time focusing on our parents' emotions to see how we need to be. Soon, we have lost track of our needs and are focusing entirely on theirs. Meanwhile, a well of emptiness and grief is building inside, out of sight. Now our struggle becomes keeping those intolerable feelings at bay by repeating the same pattern of abandoning our own needs in new relationships.

By the time we are adults, our whole system, conscious and unconscious, expects our relationships to follow this same pattern. Because all of these painful losses are still alive in us and we never developed the ability to track our own needs, we will grasp onto the nearest source of stability (usually a romantic partner) to feel safe and secure. What we learned in childhood tells us that we will need to do almost anything to keep this person by our side. It is hard to imagine any state that feels more insecure and uncertain from moment to moment, especially because even with all these efforts to take care of another person's needs, we didn't feel as though our parents were seeing us, choosing us, staying with us. This repeated loss of connection creates a stress response and awakens the sympathetic nervous system. While we believe our actions are geared toward connection, we are actually pulled out of the ventral state to our sympathetic response by our fear, which makes co-regulation and deep connection with another extremely difficult. In this agitated state, we will do anything to find some relief.

Enter the "rescue fantasy." What we need now is a savior to ride in on a white horse, scoop us up, and carry us off into the sunset. It's no wonder this fairy-tale myth is so prevalent. One of the most common ways for a child to escape the pain of abandonment by a caretaker is to create a fantasy in which we will be rescued and seen in our true worth. I worked with a young woman who shared that she imagined she could walk through the full-length mirror in her room to be with a family who cared about her. From Cinderella, to Sleeping Beauty, to Snow White, this fantasy is so commonplace, it has become deeply ingrained in the fabric of our cultural narrative.

More recently, the Twilight series glorified our infatuation with this idea, depicting how the rescue fantasy plays out in romantic relationships. Bella, the selfless maiden in distress, develops an intense love for her mysterious rescuer (in this case an exciting yet dangerous vampire). She even begs him to kill her so that they can be together forever in a shady afterlife, forsaking her human existence entirely. In this tale, it seems as though both partners have fallen into the pit of love addiction as her vampire says at one point, "You're like my own personal brand of heroin." For an anxiously attached person, the fantasy of a love that literally never dies momentarily soothes the painful subconscious belief that opening up to love will always end in loss.

As unhealthy as this fantasy might sound, the development of this storytelling Inner Protector gives us at least momentary respite from the pain of being abandoned. When attention is lacking in our family of origin, it's actually healthy that as children and adolescents, we can still imagine the possibility of being cared for and valued. The alternative is to fall into depression and despair. Seen this way, it also makes sense that we project this belief onto what we think it means to be in a loving relationship, including the idea that this person must be "the one."

Because the wound began so early, we have the inner need and expectation that this rescuer will be as fully attentive as a mother to a newborn. At the same time, we already *expect* them to abandon us—just like our caregivers did when we were most vulnerable—so we move toward *any* relationship with intense anxiety. Our primary Inner Protector was to give ourselves away, so that is what we do now as well. With few inner resources to call on, we become willing to give away all of our selves (in Bella Thorne's case, her life itself) in exchange for the love of another. As we began doing in the last chapter, we can come home to our selves when we begin to discover our Inner Nurturers and surround our selves with the outer support we need to care for our wounded Little Me until they are able to sense what they need and have the internal care system in place to ask for it.

SELFLESS, SELFISH, AND SELF-FULL

We can all embody the states of being selfless, selfish, and self-full at different times in our lives, depending on our circumstances. Some individuals tend toward one end of the spectrum over the other based on how we adapted in childhood. When you read the descriptions below, which do you most identify with? Do you find yourself feeling all of these under different circumstances? As you read through the following descriptions slowly, just notice how your body and emotions respond without judging anything that comes up as best you can.

Selfless: Selflessness stems from not having had the help to develop a sense of our own inherent worth (often blaming and shaming ourselves). In this state, we adapt to inconsistent care by coming to believe that receiving love is contingent upon giving: Namely, that we must actively not attend to our needs in order to receive love and positive attention. Often, this is easy because we no longer have much sense of what we need. We spend most of our time caring for others, and all attempts at establishing or enforcing boundaries fall apart. We are unaware or too afraid to express our own needs, which leads to us constantly feeling drained. In the selfless state, we tend to be more aware of our outer world than our inner world, often operating in a survival mode that prevents us from resting and being present with ourselves. Taking our eyes off the other person threatens to open the intolerably painful abandonment wounds. Because we have so little contact with our inner selves, we have a hard time trusting our selves, and often second-guess our decisions. Having not been able to co-regulate with our parents, being selfless also means being dependent on others to regulate us. As children, we learned to be hyperaware of the other person as a survival tactic, preventing us from embodying our core needs and emotions.

Did any memories of moments you have felt like this come up while reading this? If they did, you could write about them in your journal. If you notice bodily sensations or feelings that come with them, you could jot those down as well. These observations can become a jumping-off place for healing work with your Little Me.

Selfish: At the other end of the spectrum, we may adapt to lack of care by coming to believe that we alone are responsible for getting what we want and need. Beneath this drive to continuously have our needs met lies the same emptiness and fear as in the selfless person. All of our Inner Protectors focus exclusively on having our own needs met and can have an inflated sense of self (often blaming and shaming others). This protects us from deeply buried feelings of unworthiness. We fear being vulnerable and struggle with authentic empathy, believing that it is safer to close off to others. Sometimes, we tend to become hyper-independent to avoid relying on others to meet our needs. On the flip side, we may make unreasonable demands for what we need. Sadly, even when these demands are met, they don't fill the emptiness, so we always need more. This keeps us in a constant state of sympathetic activation. Because we are so afraid of vulnerability, we focus on relationships where we feel we have more power and control as a form of protection. We struggle with co-regulation because opening ourselves up to another feels like a threat to our sense of safety, which is built on being independent. Our boundaries can be rigid as we prefer to feel separate from others (sometimes also needing to feel special or better than). We tend to trust ourselves first and foremost and have a hard time trusting others. We learned to focus on ourselves as a way to survive and will reject the needs of others as a way of protecting ourselves from being dominated or manipulated in ways that would expose the emptiness and pain inside us.

Most of us have had some moments when we have focused only on ourselves, or we have been closely connected to others who have adapted in this way. You could write about your own moments in your journal and also about how others have affected you. It is easy to be critical of these impulses toward selfishness, but, with reflection, you will begin to see that it was pain and fear that prompted this kind of self-focus. These, too, can become places of entry into the healing work with your Little Me.

Self-full: If we have had parents who reflected our wholeness and worth, or if we have healed from childhood wounds, we have both the Inner Nurturers and outer resources to find ourselves in this state quite often. In a self-full state, we are capable of effectively meeting our own needs or asking for them to be met. We have a stable sense of self-worth and feel that we are intrinsically lovable and valuable. We are open to accepting all parts of our selves and take responsibility for our actions. We are able to maintain healthy internal and external boundaries, and have the ability to empathize with others without losing ourselves. In a state of self-fullness, we can draw on our community of Inner Nurturers to fill up with love and compassion because we have received these from others and have internalized them. This means we have ample love to give without exhausting or depleting ourselves. Because we aren't carrying a large burden of pain and fear, we feel safe to be in our bodies. This allows us to be in touch with our needs without feeling fear that they won't be met. We are able to transition between intimacy, interdependence, and autonomy in response to both internal and external conditions, without losing our sense of self. We see relationships as intrinsically interdependent and supportive, and are able to trust in others.

Writing about moments you have felt self-full in your journal, even fleetingly, will help strengthen them. You might notice the feelings that arise in your body when you focus here. Below is a chart that shows all three states and how they correlate to our ANS.

Selfless & Selfish States *Sympathetic*	Activated state of fight-or-flight Panic / fear / anxiety / worry Rage / anger / frustration Impulsiveness Expansion of energy
Self-full State *Ventral Vagal Parasympathetic*	Ability to be in connection with self and others States of joyful excitement States of deep rest Playfulness / curiosity Empathy / compassion Feeling safe
Selfless & Selfish States *Dorsal Vagal Parasympathetic*	Resignation Shame Shutting down (conserving energy) Depression Learned helplessness (when you have repeatedly tried to connect and finally collapse into despair)

As mentioned, all these states exist along a spectrum and any individual can move from one to the other. However, most of us have a tendency toward entering one of these states when we move into close relationships as a way of managing our lives. Both selfless and selfish states activate the sympathetic nervous system (fight-or-flight) and arise from fears for our survival, while the self-full state allows us to remain in the ventral state where we are more easily able to process emotions and connect with others. Gaining awareness of and having compassion and acceptance for all parts of our selves and doing the hard work of healing whatever core wounds we are carrying is what supports ongoing development of a self-full state.

IDEALIZING AND LOVE-BOMBING

If you identify as anxiously attached, it's very likely that the rescue fantasy rings true for you. Perhaps it's a dynamic that's been playing on repeat in your life without you even realizing, as you subconsciously idolize new partners as potential rescuers only to have them actually leave you feeling even more lost and alone. This is also extremely common, and we see it play out in the anxious-avoidant dance described in previous chapters.

If we are children who never had the experience of our caregivers' undivided, adoring attention, we will still be yearning inside for that feeling of being swaddled in constant unconditional love. Often, this idealization begins with parents and other caregivers who have (often unknowingly) abandoned and wounded us. When we are very small, our just-developing brains experience a blissful sense of mother when she is available and a painful, frightening sense of mother when she is not. If our parents are there for us enough in early childhood these two states blend into us being able to experience people as whole—with flaws and with delightful strengths. We experience ourselves that way, too. When our parents aren't able to be there with us with warmth, care, and acceptance, the ache for the perfect person who will be totally available is never filled. There remains in us a felt need for someone to be that perfect for us.

When a potential partner comes toward us with this kind of attention—which some call *love bombing*—Little Me begins to feel that their savior has appeared because we have yearned for this since infancy. Whether in the form of compliments, tokens of affection, love notes, or promises of the whole moon, whether well-intended or not, our Little Me parts who have protected themselves with a rescue fantasy are going to feel like we have finally found our savior. Now we will begin to idealize our new love interest, believing that our partner can do no wrong and setting ourselves up to forgive or overlook any shortcomings. As the need for this bond continues to grow, we begin to lose sight of our own needs and interests. Soon, Little Me will do whatever it takes to keep this person as we become steadily more selfless.

Part of the tragedy here is that the initial phase of a relationship often involves this kind of complete focus on each other, and as the relationship matures, it will naturally become less. Constant attention to each other gives way to life's needs. If things are going well, we develop more trust and this begins to lessen the need for constant reassurance. If our Little Me is still so wounded from early life experience, it is often impossible for them to make that transition. Instead, Little Me becomes more frightened and gives more of themselves away to try to keep the intensity going.

Because parts of Little Me have not been given what they needed to develop a sense of self, in the extreme, this relationship can lead to a desire to enmesh entirely with a partner because being encircled with the energy of the other person feels like the only place they are safe, just like a baby. Any time these wounded aspects of Little Me sense a threat to this security, their internal alarm system goes off. They become obsessive about maintaining closeness with their partner, directing all their focus, energy, and attention toward them, which could lead to scooping out any last reserves of self-respect. To make matters worse, if their partner has adapted by developing avoidant tendencies, this clinging will only push him or her further away, so the partner begins to respond with a need for distance to feel safe. The partner may stop returning calls or disappear altogether, for example. If this is painfully familiar, it's important to know that there is no shame in these behaviors or feelings. Your Little Me is trying to establish closeness because they sense a threat to survival. Simply becoming aware of this when it is happening is the first step to learning how to intervene when you slip into this state.

The rescuer myth seeks to protect our abandonment wounds, but sadly it is this very fantasy that keeps so many people clinging to pain-filled and even abusive relationships. The ingrained idea that being selfless is a virtue and that others' needs must always come before our own only compounds the problem. With the work we are doing, our Little Me will discover that they have internal resources in the form of Nurturers and external resources in trustworthy people now. From there, the rescue fantasy will lose its appeal because it is no longer needed.

HUNGRY FOR LOVE

The selfless state can show up in a magnified way in a concept known as *love hunger* or emotional hunger. When people have been very deprived of love, they can literally develop the desire to "consume" the object of their affection. One of my clients, grieving the demise of her last relationship, said she was experiencing extreme withdrawal from what had been a case of acute love addiction. "I miss him so much I just want to *eat* him," she told me, language you might have heard before or even used yourself.

For anyone, especially someone who is avoidant, can you imagine how smothering it feels to be on the other side of a need like this? But it is simply Little Me expressing the extent to which they feel they NEED the love of another, in order to fill the emptiness they feel inside. Just like physical hunger, this sensation can even manifest as a physical "ache" for another person's attention, and very real "cravings" for their touch. The same way feelings of emptiness can lead to emotional overeating, "love hunger" can lead us to "bingeing" on relationships that will never completely fill us because, in fact, we can only be satisfied by becoming self-full and in the care of our Inner Nurturers.

It took us months of inner work to bathe her wounded Little Me in the care she needed from having lost her mother to an illness when she was two months old. At that age, food and love are intertwined in a way that if a child loses her primary person, she will feel starving and cold even if her basic needs are being met. We built her community of Inner Nurturers, beginning with the two of us, and then expanded to a broader circle of trustworthy friends, exactly the process a baby goes through from birth through the first year of life. Gradually, her cravings for her ex began diminishing as she was taking in the care surrounding her. Her active choice to commit to her healing, first and foremost, gave her emotional void the abundance it had always needed, and eventually she was able to move on.

OFF THE PEDESTAL

Stella is a client who came to me confused about why she was attracting the same kind of guy over and over again—highly successful and powerful men often preoccupied with their business ventures. They were also all married. Stella herself is bright and intelligent, and she didn't understand why she kept attracting men who were obviously unavailable.

After exploring her past, it became clear that the men she was attracted to all had similar traits to her father, a man she idealized as if he were superhuman. He was very successful and also viewed any sign of sadness as a vulnerability and therefore a weakness. She also shared that her father's father had been a tough guy, pushing his sons around to make sure they behaved like "little men" by the time they were three years old. We paused, feeling how her father's wounds kept him from acknowledging any pain or softness in himself or anyone else.

She began to harden herself on the outside to remain in his favor. Inside, she buried her softer feelings side by side with the pain of not being acknowledged as the family pattern embedded itself in her generation. Stella also shared that her father remarried when she was twelve, and that it was very clear that he valued his new wife above everyone else. She spent some sessions sharing about how unchosen she felt, feeling abandoned by her father for many years. It was also very hard for her to express any anger around how her father behaved, since his aura of invincibility demanded that she place him on a pedestal. She needed a father even if it meant giving herself up, and he needed a daughter who would help protect him from his own vulnerable wound by abandoning herself. Unable to see him as the bad guy, she subconsciously blamed herself for the way he treated her.

It was clear to me that her abandonment wound was being reenacted in her adult relationships, both by choosing men who were so invested in success they had little interest in their own emotions, much less hers, and pursuing married men who weren't going to leave their wives. If only one of these men would choose her, she might feel worthy. This inevitably backfired. Every time one of them didn't choose her, her deepest knowing would be further cemented in place: *I am not interesting, I am not enough, and I will never be a priority.*

Our work together focused on Stella getting back in touch with many aspects of her Little Me. She had yearned to have her father notice when she was sad or upset. Her twelve-year-old Little Me felt the anguish of seeing all her father's attention directed at this new wife. In my office, with me being the presence of her Inner Nurturers, she was finally able to express some anger toward her father, and to validate these feelings as natural and okay. Toppled from his pedestal, she saw him as he is, a flawed human being who loved his daughter the only way he knew how and, in the process, let her down over and over again. Over a period of time, she worked up the courage to hold space for her sadness as well, as she came to understand that welcoming and accepting all her feelings—no matter how painful—was part of her becoming self-full. Ultimately, by becoming connected to her own emotional experience, receiving the caring attention and validation from me and others that she had never had, and embracing her full self in this way, she attracted an emotionally available partner.

It is so normal for our Little Me to idealize our abandoner, the way Stella idealized her father. Often, this means we will only remember the good times because those are the moments we felt briefly met. The pain and fear get pushed far out of conscious awareness so we can continue to move forward in life. Then we anxiously wait for the precious good moments to return in each relationship. Every time they come back in the form of a potential love interest, we may feel temporarily soothed, only to face disappointment as this person can't heal the deeper wounds. When we find the support to work with our Little Me parts and build an inner community of support, we will be sturdier and more balanced as we move toward a new partner.

♥♥

SURRENDERING TO THE TRUST FALL

Imagine you are standing with your back to a group of people you trust will catch you when you deliberately fall back toward them. You must feel enough safety to truly let go and fall into their arms. You let go and you are indeed caught. Releasing the rescue fantasy is like this. For those of us who are anxiously attached, surrendering the story that has kept us safe from our deep feelings of abandonment requires inner and outer reassurances that we will be caught by something that will provide true safety and true connection. This doesn't happen all at once, but as our Little Me heals more deeply and as we continue to build a community of Inner Nurturers, there will be a letting go. For now, the intention to surrender the rescue fantasy is enough. That commitment asks you to trust that falling into your fear of being alone, with strong and tender inner and outer support, is taking the next step toward healing. It takes courage to go down this path because the first time you were so trusting and vulnerable as a baby or young child, this openness brought pain that is still with you.

That we are carrying these old wounds is half of the story of what it is to be human. The other half is that we also carry undeveloped resources of health in every cell and every neural pathway. Working through our pain makes room for this inherent health to emerge. From the spiritual viewpoint, we might call this *awareness of connection to a higher Source*. What if we were able to experience a deeper truth than the compelling feeling of insecurity we learned as children? It might be possible to heal enough of the fear to experience the love and support that is available to us, right here, right now. When we are able to do that, our hearts open, and we begin to see that we are and always have been supported every step of the way, by our friendships, our own creativity and ingenuity, and even by nature itself. The whole time Little Me has been attaching to others in an attempt to feel whole, their earliest learnings have blinded them to the simple truth of the universe: They are already intrinsically connected to all that is. In the throes of abandonment terror, this deeper and truer way of seeing can feel like it is the fantasy, but as we heal enough to let go of the story of rescue, we will get closer to this sense of being held.

We'll explore this process further in chapter 8. For now, I want you to consider surrender as an active step away from self-abandonment and toward a deep, fulfilling, and unshakable connection with your inner self. You've come this far, and I know from personal experience how exhausted you are from the chasing, the worry, the self-sacrifice, and the bending over backward for relationships that are draining your soul. Living in a selfless state means you so often feel depleted. No amount of spa days or retail therapy can replenish the energy flowing out in your wounded attempts to find and keep hold of love.

As scary as it may sound to begin to let go of everything you were taught about how to love and be loved, I am also living proof of the freedom and inner peace that awaits you on the other side. Watching my clients take this journey and experience what is essentially a coming home to themselves is the reason I do the work that I do.

As we have learned, this begins with returning to and tending your own inner world. Part of this work is healing the wounds our Little Me has sustained, which we began in the last chapter. Here, we are going to continue that work and also focus on building your capacity to sense more of who you truly are beneath and beyond these wounds. With the Self-full Meditation below, you and I will journey more deeply into Little Me's world. All of their emotions will be welcomed, while your Inner Nurturers will remind you of your wholeness, and nurture a gradually expanding sense of inner calm and groundedness. We will be able to move toward experiencing warm emotions, such as gratitude, joy, empathy, and love in the here and now.

When we experience uplifting emotions such as these, our heart rhythm pattern becomes highly ordered, resembling a smooth, harmonious wave. This is called *coherence* and, with practice, we are able to generate this relaxed but awake state for ourselves more often. The heart and the mind become synchronized, giving us more access to the loving, intuitive voice and helping us feel more connected to our innate wisdom. In this state, we will feel safer, and that increases the amount of time we are spending in the ventral state where we can experience a greater sense of self-fullness and connect more easily with others.

This meditation is also designed to help you relax enough to shift your brain waves from beta to alpha. This allows you to slow down and relax to the point that you are able to gain access to more of your subconscious mind. This is where you do the healing work with Little Me that will gradually shift any feelings and beliefs you may hold about your overall lack of worth. As we do this work, we are also providing what is needed to change your attachment system from anxious to secure. This happens because you will be receiving what your system needed but wasn't available when you were small.

This is the essential food you have needed to develop a sense of security in yourself.

Before we begin, we should journey back to chapter 2 and take note of the memories, feelings, and beliefs that you uncovered there. Setting an intention, which simply means making a conscious commitment to return to a particular way of being with this practice, can help. One that fits with what we have been doing is *I am supported.* When we work on becoming self-full, we are essentially building trust in both our inner and outer resources and the universe itself to be able to give us what we need.

I will be your companion in this deeply restorative meditation. Together, we will guide your mind into a state where you are ready to let go into the trust and fall toward the pain and the healing. This is very deep work, and it will be more effective the more you practice. Any new state of being requires repetition to build sturdy new neural pathways. If you can, set aside some time to repeat this exercise every day as you cultivate a sense of your wholeness. Gradually, the inherent worthiness that is your birthright will become clear to you. Trust me—even if you don't buy into it fully now, your future self is already thanking you!

DAILY PRACTICE: SELF-FULL MEDITATION

Now we are going to deepen into the healing process of Little Me as well as strengthen the connection with our Inner Nurturers and make room for your Inner Protectors to be less on guard. No matter how you are feeling in this moment, you can keep in mind that every neural system in your body has its own kind of inherent health. For example, your muscles have the capacity to relax. At the same time, these systems have also adapted to the pain and fear you have experienced. They hold the felt sense memories of those events. In your muscles, these are areas of chronic tension. No matter how many massages you get or how many relaxation exercises you practice, these muscles get tense again because they are asking you to attend to the deeper meaning of the tension. They hold aspects of Little Me that want to be seen, held, and acknowledged.

Here, you and I are going to gently approach your wise body because it carries both the wounds and the pathway to healing. Listening to it illuminates that pathway. I will be guiding you along as you attune to your muscles and the space around them, your belly, and your heart, opening to their stories and inviting your community of Inner Nurturers to hold a warm, steady space as I help you find your way back to the abundant inherent health that has always been with you. Then we will focus on filling up with feelings of support as you tap into your heart and feel the earth's loving support below you. One of the beauties of doing this practice is that the heart-brain produces oxytocin, the hormone that is released when we feel loving trust for someone. As we work through the stored energy and allow that to be released, we begin to create uplifting emotions from within. Accessing these warm emotions in our heart center allows us to create these neurochemicals intentionally, becoming our own inner pharmacy.

Since it's wise to move slowly into this practice, set aside about thirty to forty minutes for the extended recorded version and about twenty minutes for the meditation below. The meditation can be done in stages or all at once, depending on time or how you are feeling that day. There will be cues given at the end of each section to indicate where you can choose either to carry on or close your practice for the day. These cues will be at the end of the muscle sensing and relaxation parts. Belly releasing, the final section, is heart expansion and will be the bringing together of the whole mediation experience.

To begin, find a safe place where you will not be interrupted. The recorded, extended version of this meditation is at **beselffull .com/meditations**, and you may find that following my voice will help you let go and also remind you that we are doing this together. You are also welcome to share this experience with a trusted friend or your therapist for additional support.

Gather some pillows and blankets to get cozy. Lying on the floor can help you feel supported by the earth. It can feel extra supportive to have something under your knees to release the lower back and maybe a small pillow under your head. Just as in seated meditation, you'll want to accommodate having a neutral spine and feeling balanced and at ease in the body. Here you are invited to let go and relax. Be sure to turn off any distractions. Each of the steps listed below is merely a suggestion, and if you don't feel like going into any of the areas I mention, then please listen to yourself and go at your own pace.

As we begin, I will be asking your awareness to pay attention to particular parts of your body. When you attempt to do that, it is normal and natural for your mind to wander. As much as possible, try not to be judgmental about this. Instead, a gentle encouragement for your mind to return to focusing your attention back to your breath is all that is needed. You may sense the voice of your Inner Nurturers helping with this. Here we go.

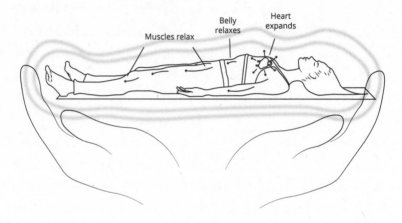

1. Once you are feeling safe, comfortable, and undistracted, allow yourself to feel supported by the ground beneath you. Even if you are lying in your bed, you can feel the body of the earth holding your body. You can put an eye mask on if that feels comfortable.

2. Relax your breathing and start to feel and become aware of your breath entering your body. Breathe into your belly 360 degrees, and sense your breath entering every cell, traveling down every limb, and washing in waves over your heart. Notice any areas where the breath finds it harder to enter. Just notice without judgment. Your breath is guiding you to places of ease and places that need attention. As much as you are able in this moment, fill your body with breath

and feel it expand your inner world, and then release it out through your mouth. Do this slowly, being aware of any feelings that come up as you slow down and begin to deepen.

3. Continuing to breathe in this way, give yourself full permission to be here with your body just as it is right now. Begin to notice that the breath is something that is both outside of you and simultaneously within you so that you are never void of support. Gently scan your body for parts that might be holding tension. Perhaps you can feel some tightness in your shoulders, hips, or jaw. Anywhere you feel tension, pause to see if this muscle is holding something it wishes to share. Imagine a softening around the part that is holding tension. When you sense that the muscle is ready for you to move on, gently send your breath into that area and ask if it is ready to release what it has been holding on to. Allow for ten breaths, sending them into places that you feel are holding tension.

4. Now you're going to begin to deepen your awareness of some parts of your body in turn. When you approach with a listening heart, your body has the opportunity to share its wisdom. You may get a sense that this part is at ease or troubled. In either case, it is holding something. Remembering the intention—*I am supported*—offers space in which what is held may emerge. It will usually start as a sensation that may then become an emotion, a memory, an intuitive knowing of something sweet or painful. All of this is the voice of your Little Me parts, telling you the story of where they have felt

supported and where they have felt abandoned. Most of us aren't used to listening in this way, so please be gentle and accepting of yourself, however this may unfold. Such kindness is the presence of your Inner Nurturers reminding you of how much you are loved and how completely accepted you are whether you do this exercise just right or not.

5. Focus on muscles in particular areas that frequently hold tension: your legs, your arms and shoulders, your back, your neck and jaw, and the area around your eyes. Let's begin by inviting your attention to drop down to your legs. You arrive there simply to listen, not to change anything. This is so important because it makes room for your body to share its wisdom, to share Little Me's story as it is held in your muscles. You can notice that there may be areas of relaxation and areas of tension. Then you might sense if there are particular parts of your legs that call for your attention. When your mind comes to rest there, you can be open to whatever that muscle is wanting to share. The language of the body is *sensation*, so just beginning to attend to that is to begin listening to the story your body is holding. As you pay attention here, it is possible that the sensation will change. It may decrease or intensify. A memory of a past experience may come to mind. Emotions may arise—sadness, joy, confusion, peace, anger—anything from the whole range of human feelings. As you are receptive to each of these tender communications, you may feel a sense of gratitude emerging—maybe both from you and from the muscle whose story you are witnessing.

6. When you have a sense that the muscles in your legs feel heard, you can begin to focus on your breath, sending gentle inhalations and exhalations of gratitude for the conversation. Even with these breaths, there is no intention to get your muscles to do anything different but simply to offer them the gift of thanks.

7. Now you can repeat this process with your arms and shoulders. Focus, listening, receiving whatever stories are shared, offering the breath of gratitude.

8. And then to your back.

9. And then to your neck and jaw.

10. And then to the area around your eyes.

11. Now it's time to invite your attention to your belly. It can be really helpful to place one or both hands on your belly, sensing where they would like to rest. Your belly-brain actually extends all the way up to the notch of your collarbone, so if your hands feel drawn there, you can just follow them. You arrive here only to listen, not to direct. Remembering that *sensation* is the language of the body, you can begin to notice the feeling that your belly is offering you right now. There are so many cultural dictates about how the size and shape of bellies are supposed to be that this may be the first layer of response. You might hear "You are too big." You might hear

"I don't like you." If that arises, sense how your belly responds to these messages. Focus back on filling your belly with your inhalation and deeply letting go with your exhalation. Spend about ten breaths here.

12. See if it's possible to listen more deeply now. You might ask, "What do you have to share with me today?" You can receive whatever is offered—which may be a lot or nothing at all this time. Sometimes the "nothing at all" is a sense of ease letting us know that there is safety in this moment. If instead you feel tightening or butterflies, you can stay with it and see what wants to unfold from there. As with your muscles, memories, emotions, or more sensations may come. As best you can, stay in receptivity with the support of your Inner Nurturers, who offer comfort and reassurance. Maybe you can even sense yourself letting go as if all that support is right under you, catching you as you relax even deeper into the earth below you.

13. Now, send three deep breaths into your belly while offering it thanks. This belly is the guardian of your safety, the digester of your food, and the support for your immune system. It holds memories of the beautiful times that support your sense of hope and goodness in relationships. It also holds memories of the times of pain and struggle so that these can heal. As you fill your belly with breath, offer these words: "I will always listen. You will always be supported." Spend about ten breaths here.

14. Begin now to notice your breath and guide it down and around your heart space. With each inhalation, you collect the breath, and with each exhalation, you send the breath to your heart. You will stay here and just send about ten to twenty breaths into this space, allowing some feelings of gratitude for your heart as it continues to beat for you. Maybe you hear the beat. Maybe you can visualize your heart as you continue to direct your breath to this area. Your heart is your intuitive center and it also holds the pain from heartbreak as well as wisdom and joy about connection. As you're breathing, see if your heart is ready to soften. Relax into your heart space with each breath.

15. Now it's time to connect to your community of Inner Nurturers. Connect once again with the symbolism of the breath being both outside and within you simultaneously. Your Inner Nurturers also exist like your breath both inside and outside of you. Let's think of one person who has loved and supported you, and focus on inviting their warm, nurturing support to be present with you. As this supportive presence radiates within you, it can be natural to feel an emergence of emotion connected to this unconditional support. Maybe you have a visual or perhaps you feel the warmth that this energy brings around you.

16. See if you can sense your Inner Nurturer seeing you. They are lovingly noticing you, seeing how much you have been through, how much you have struggled. They see your joy

and your pain, holding all of it with you. They know how hard you have worked to survive. They are now letting you know you can trust and let go because you have them and the earth right below you, supporting you. You can let go with a little more trust as you feel the ground below you, holding you, reminding you that you will always be supported. Begin to feel how we have both inner and outer support always coexisting, the earth's nurturing hands forever holding you in love. Perhaps you can allow the notion of never being alone start to find a light within you.

17. Practice inhaling the feelings of support and warmth of the earth as you think of a particular Inner Nurturer. It can even be a pet or a time when you remember feeling free and supported. Inhale as you collect that energy and pass it through your whole body with that feeling. You might imagine yourself filling up with that felt sense of warmth and support, and let it cycle through your body with each inhalation and exhalation. We will stay here for ten breaths while you practice feeling that support move through your whole body. Allow yourself to open to receiving warmth, nurturing, and care. Spend as long as you need here, sensing into your heart space.

18. It may help you to focus if you place a hand or two on your chest, sensing where it feels just right. When you feel you have arrived, listen to the sensations in your heart and chest. You might say, "What do you wish to share with me right

now?" Emotions, memories, sensations may come. As best you can, receive whatever is offered, trusting the wisdom of the heart. If painful memories or feelings come, offer comfort and reassurance to your Little Me. What they are sharing is a precious gift.

19. When it feels as though your heart is finished sharing for this day, take several breaths into your heart and ask if it has anything else it would like to share with Little Me, or perhaps a message just for you. Spend a couple of breaths just to see if anything comes up. You might even sense a whisper coming through your heart that is guiding you.

20. As we prepare to finish this meditation, you can widen your awareness to include the whole body and send three deep breaths into your muscles, your belly, and your heart, while offering this precious wise body thanks. Spend as long as you need in any gratitude you might feel right now just for being here with yourself in such a kind way.

21. To close, slowly come back up to a supported seated position, then remove your eye mask, keeping your eyes closed, as you come back into the room.

22. Open your eyes, stretch, and feel back into the physical world by taking a moment to notice the details of the room. Our journey is complete for today.

You might want to spend some time journaling or drawing afterward. There is no particular format for this. Just allow whatever words or images that come to you to flow onto the paper. You may also feel a little spacey and like you need some quiet time to simply be with whatever came up. Take as much extra time for this as you need, and please be gentle with yourself. If your Inner Protectors urge you to do something other than what you sense you need, simply notice them and let them know you've got this. The key is not to analyze the experience too deeply, or to try to make sense of what comes up. Simply allow it all to be, and continue practicing this meditation regularly. You will find it is different each time as you access more and more of Little Me's experience with the ever-growing support of your Inner Nurturers. Doing this practice regularly will release more of the old pain and deepen your access to the presence of your Inner Nurturers.

I imagine you are beginning to get the sense that support is everything on this path of healing. We each have inner resources from those who have cared for us in the past, outer resources from those trustworthy others who are with us on the path, and also what we might call *divine resources*—stemming from our connection to the loving universe. All of these resources combine to become the presence and voice of our Inner Nurturer community, which is growing stronger within you each day. A trustworthy friend or two, a therapist, and a spiritual teacher or guide can all offer the kind of nonjudgmental listening that helps build a secure home base for this work.

It is through the felt sense of being supported that Little Me lets subconscious memories surface. By giving them what they needed but did not receive at the time, old wounds will begin to heal. In terms of your brain, your amygdala is more and more supported by your middle prefrontal cortex, creating feelings of safety and being cared for. We could say that your Inner Nurturers live both in your heart and right in the midst of that feeling of being held while you heal. Before, your amygdala was on high alert, anticipating each fresh abandonment. Now, you will find you have more space to think and to calm yourself down when you are activated. Best of all, as you continue to heal in this way, you are rewiring Little Me's relationship expectations. This begins with a different felt sense of what relationship can be, leading to a shift in subconscious beliefs about what it means to be in partnership. Over time, you will find that your conscious thoughts about your own worth and what it means to give and receive love also begin to shift.

Being with yourself in the present moment through listening to your body and holding space with compassion for your whole self is medicine for the psyche. It is how you will begin to relate to the world from a healing inner awareness instead of having external experiences stir up Little Me's wounds and guide your feelings and behavior.

In essence, doing this work means making an inner commitment to yourself that is the ultimate antidote to the inner abandonment that leads to selflessness, codependency, and love addiction. While the results are nothing short of miraculous, if at first it seems like things are actually getting more destabilized, trust that this is because you're in transition. At these moments, having others nearby who support you—and that includes me—is essential. Your Inner Nurturers gain strength both from your own inner depths and from internalizing others' deep, heartfelt care and attention. You may have heard this transformational process referred to as a "dark night of the soul"—something with which I am so familiar.

I used to think that "doing the work" looked like some chic woman meditating like a tranquil Buddha on a snowcapped mountaintop. I imagined others who had found this path as being a mix of badass and perfectly put-together; a cross between Beyoncé and Julia Roberts with a sprinkle of the edginess from someone like Ruby Rose. When you see a woman like this on social media, radiating inner peace and self-empowerment, you probably feel like you'll never be as cool and as effortlessly self-assured as she is. But this woman *is* you. Behind the glossy filters, everyone has times when they feel like everything is falling apart, and times that are painful and hard. Finding our own embodied sense of personal power can only come from taking an honest look inward, something that is never going to be all light and love. This is the part that nobody wants to share, and that's okay. The messy, uncomfortable process of mining layers of uncharted territory within yourself is not for show or for public consumption. This deeply personal work can only be felt on the inside and shared with those caring and trustworthy others you've invited.

When I first started looking at my own issues with codependency and love addiction, I went through a period of depression. I knew I could no longer try to hide out in my relationships, and so I had to confront my abandonment issues head-on. I had spent my whole life avoiding being with myself, and as painful as it was, I knew I had to spend some time with my inner world and all it contained. My heart was heavy as I deeply connected to the sense of loneliness I experienced as a child, I also allowed my therapist to be present with me while I connected to the sensations of heaviness and pressure in my heart. As I worked through my fears about not being lovable and my shame around not being good enough, I just kept recommitting to myself. I would repeat "I love you" a lot to myself during this time. At first, this actually felt awful, as if these were just empty words I knew weren't true, but over time I was able to believe this, and to feel the warmth from my words cycle through my energetic system. I began to feel my heart open, and eventually going inward started to feel amazing. I also stopped focusing on finding "the one" to complete me and focused on building connections with the people who were the most present, available, and nurturing in my life. Remember, all of this takes time, it takes practice, and it cannot be forced, so please be kind to yourself. If you hit a block, know that this is completely normal, and simply stay committed to yourself. Healing core wounds is like running a marathon while rewiring your whole house. It is *so* much work, and you so deserve to have others with you for support throughout every part of the process.

And trust me: The day will come when you finally feel accepting of your whole self. I still remember to this day realizing that I no longer wanted to be someone else. At that moment, I stopped seeing everyone else as having their life completely together and was able to see that we are all simply doing our best to love and be loved. This was when I started to fully embrace my own existence as my unique opportunity to grow and evolve, and to hold space for myself in this process, no matter what. While the accompaniment of others on this path has so enriched my process, I also do my part by remaining fully committed to the work of becoming more and more myself.

Everyone who's picked up this book will be at a different stage in this unique process. And while it's true that the more pain and trauma you have experienced throughout your life, the harder this process may be, please don't be discouraged if at first it feels like it's not working. Or if you are discouraged, maybe you can feel me with you as a comforting presence. If you were sitting here in my office right now, I would look you in the eyes and let you know: "You are supported more than you can believe, and you are not alone." So please keep trying, keep trusting, and keep recommitting to yourself.

3

Loving with Our Whole Self

CHAPTER 7

The Beauty of Boundaries

One of the new capacities you will be discovering as you heal is that it is possible to establish healthy boundaries that are neither solid walls nor open doors. They grow out of and support mutual respect between people, reflecting that each person's needs matter. For most of us who are anxiously attached, this could be a new experience. Because of the conditions of childhood, we developed a beautiful sensitivity to the needs of others at the expense of attending to our own. Our parents weren't able to help us define a clear sense of our selves because they needed us to care for their wounded Little Mes by focusing on them. No one is at fault because our parents likely didn't get what they needed, either, but the result is a deeply embedded pattern of putting others first.

Having better boundaries will not mean shutting down your

capacity to love and be loved. It will not mean issuing threats and ultimatums, or making a knee-jerk decision to break up with somebody the first time he or she upsets you. Rather, it is about doubling down on healing to become more self-full, so that fear of losing your relationship doesn't keep you from exploring what it is like to balance your needs with those of another. One truth is that in order to have a healthy "we," you must first establish a distinct "me." In addition, in order to develop a distinct "me," you need to be in relationship with people whose own healthy "me" lets you experience what it is like to be part of a nourishing "we." Co-regulation at its best! As you have been drawing trustworthy people into your healing circle and as your relationship with your Inner Nurturers is strengthening, you are having more opportunities to explore how flexible boundaries actually make relationships more safe by providing for the needs of both people.

DEVELOPING INNER BOUNDARIES

All of us have two kinds of boundaries—inner and outer. It isn't just a matter of deciding what we will and won't tolerate, and then letting our partners know. Those are outer boundaries and rest on our ability to sense what is okay and not okay for us, which is one of the outcomes of the deep healing work we're doing.

So how do inner boundaries develop? During our early years, we are constantly looking to our parents and other caregivers for a response that reflects what is going on inside us. If I am feeling angry and my mother says, "Oh, sweetie, you look really mad right now," I feel seen and accepted just as I am. I am learning that my needs are legitimate and that I can trust myself to know what I need. This is the solid foundation on which inner boundaries rest. However, if my parents look upset at my anger and turn away, I begin to sense there is something wrong with that feeling. My need to connect with the people closest to me is much stronger than my need to know myself, and so if this happens over and over, I tuck that feeling away as "bad" because it disrupts my connection with my most important people. I also begin to watch them more carefully for signs that I have upset them and then do whatever I need to soothe them to get them to stay in connection. Rather than trusting that I know what I need, I establish a deep pattern of giving myself away to maintain the relationship, so I have no sense of healthy boundaries at all.

For other children, their parents may have been able to attend to most of their emotions, but a few were off-limits. For example, if a mom is generally loving and attentive but can't tolerate when her baby turns away to rest because of her *own* abandonment wounds, she will try to force the child to reconnect. What the baby learns is that she must not rest or she will lose her connection with her mom. Perhaps you can feel how this could lead to her becoming an adult who feels comfortable with most of her own feelings but has an ingrained pattern that says she must always be available in her relationships, even if she is exhausted, even if her partner is more than willing for her to have space when she needs it. She might be able to say, "No, I don't want a beer right now," but not be able to say, "I'd really rather not go miniature golfing tonight," even though she's so tired. Most of us have certain areas where we struggle with boundaries and areas where we are solidly aware of our needs and can speak for them.

It would be helpful to sit with these last few paragraphs and see if you can begin to sense which of your emotions were reflected accurately and with care by each early caregiver, and which were frowned on or disavowed. What does it feel like in your body when you are lovingly validated? What about when you feel an emotion is unacceptable?

There is also another process at work here. With our parents, we need to develop a clear sense of who we are *separate from them*. For example, any time we cry and somebody notices and responds to us, we begin to understand that our actions have an impact on others—in this case, because they come to help us. Aha! If they were not separate from us, they would be crying in distress, too. However, if our primary caregiver *is* visibly experiencing her own distress, not only is she unable to respond to our needs, we may even begin to absorb her feelings and her struggles as if they are our own. Because she doesn't experience a felt sense of mother and child as two separate individuals, she will struggle to form a clear sense of herself as separate from others as an adult, too. This can happen with friends, work partners, lovers, and our own children.

In addition to all of this, we are also internalizing the presence of our early caregivers. When it goes well, these loving, attentive beings become the first voices of our Inner Nurturer community. This allows us to develop the ability to detach physically from our caregivers while remaining in emotional contact with them *because they remain part of us*. But of course, we also internalize our anxiety-inducing parents, so their inner presence continues to provoke fear even when we aren't physically with them.

In short, the safer we felt being *dependent* as children, the greater our ability to form healthy *interdependence* with flexible boundaries as adults because we learned to trust what we need and feel and were helped to experience ourselves as a valuable individual separate from our parents. By the same token, the less we felt like we could depend on our caregivers, the more likely we will be to struggle with both separation *and* connection because we lose our inner boundaries and give ourselves away when we're afraid we're going to lose our relationships. One way to try to maintain this sense of deep connection to another is by being consumed by the feelings and the needs of our lover and their Little Me, just as we did with our parents in childhood.

Without the felt sense of a boundary on the inside, we won't be able to have clear, flexible boundaries on the outside. We can't help but become emotionally enmeshed with our partner when we haven't developed a secure sense of self. It isn't as simple as telling people what healthy boundaries look like because the patterning we learned goes so deep and is so compelling. I so often see my clients drop everything to tend exclusively to their partner's needs at the slightest sign of them lacking something or being in emotional distress without even being aware it is happening. At other times, rather than working to alleviate the distress, they are swept up in their partner's emotional tidal wave. For example, when one client's partner lost his job, she spiraled into depression with him, just as she had with her mother. Without healing, it is a hard cycle to break because our Little Me parts believe in the deepest part of themselves that this is the only way to stay in connection. They believe that if they take care of their partner, they are more likely to be taken care of in return. At an even deeper level, they have also experienced that their best attempts didn't always bring their caregivers to them, so they are always ready to redouble their efforts and do better than their best. This is exhausting and perpetuates high levels of anxiety. Without healing, it is still preferable to the excruciating feelings of abandonment that well up if they stop trying.

Of course, we can and should hold space with empathy for our partner, but from a place of being self-full enough to balance this with space and empathy for our own needs as well. When this is reciprocated by our partner, we have the foundation for a relationship that can help each person heal and grow on their way to fulfilling, long-lasting intimacy. I'm here to tell you that by doing the work of becoming self-full, you can look forward to navigating boundaries in a way that allows for feelings of both support and freedom in your relationship without feeling anxious.

INTERDEPENDENCE, NOT INDEPENDENCE

After not having had boundaries for so long, as we begin to do our healing work, the pendulum can swing the other way. As we get more of a sense of ourselves as separate, with our own needs and wants, we can have a tendency to believe that becoming strong, independent people who don't need anybody is both the goal and the ultimate safety. Certain forces in our culture may support this. While it can feel like a powerful way to live after giving ourselves up for so long, simply throwing up a wall is actually another form of self-protection rather than an invitation into sustainable intimacy. We may be thinking, "Well, now I can't be hurt because I'm not going to let anyone near me." Soon we begin to notice that we feel just as lonely as before. Rather than a solid brick wall, the kind of boundary I'm talking about is more like a gateway that opens and closes.

The goal here is not to become so good at being on our own that we don't need anybody, but rather to be in a healthy, *fluid* relationship with others. Connection is what we're wired for, after all, and while single life can be a lot of fun, ultimately people are meant to be in warm, caring relationships. According to some solid research, we have evolved to *expect* to be in connection and suffer internally if we're not, even if we're not consciously aware of the feelings brought on by aloneness. So how do we anxiously attached people get to the place where we can fall into love without drowning? Not surprisingly, the answer is investing in healing. The beautiful paradox is that the more we have a secure sense of our own self, the more we can throw our selves fully into a loving relationship with a partner without getting lost.

This is very different from codependency, where our feelings and behaviors in relationships are driven by fear, not trust. If we come to rely on our partners as our sole source of comfort, stability, and love, this dynamic quickly becomes stagnant and unfulfilling. *Interdependent* relationships, on the other hand, allow space for each partner to grow and evolve in his or her own ways, without the other person feeling threatened by this. This is the bedrock of longevity and ever-deepening intimacy between lovers. But it requires inner security, trust, and an ability to navigate the transitions of togetherness and separateness without either person being swallowed up in feelings of being invaded or abandoned. It also means being able to trust that after the inevitable disagreements that happen in all relationships, there can also be repair. And that these repairs actually strengthen the connection. Clear inner boundaries help us sense our own needs and feel comfortable sharing them with our partners, and we don't feel threatened by our partners having different needs than us. We can negotiate how these needs will be met and make the necessary compromises without losing our sense of self. The other part of this is that when each of us takes responsibility for his or her own feelings, actions, and contributions to the relationship, there is sufficient solidity in both people for it to be safe to become increasingly close as well.

WHY ANGER IS IMPORTANT

As our inner boundaries become clear, we can begin to consider what outer boundaries might look like. Before that inner clarity comes, our wounded Little Me often has trouble acting on boundaries even if they think they are a good idea. It's simply too threatening.

We're going to begin with a boundary that society often considers off-limits, especially for women—*anger*. It's helpful to understand that all of our emotions are messengers with something important to say to us and to others. So, what is the message of anger? Anger is an important communication about our pain, and often shows us where a boundary has been crossed or where we need to set a boundary. If you really explore your anger, often what you will find is feelings of being hurt or scared. Anger becomes a cue into many emotions that help us gain awareness around unmet needs, fears, and pain.

We all have some brain circuitry in our spine at the back of our neck, right below our hairline, that wakes up when we have tried to connect over and over but no one is available for us. A baby in her crib will whimper, then cry, then escalate to red-faced, vibrating rage when she is left alone in distress. This is a healthy response that says, "You are hurting me. Why won't you come, why won't you come, why won't you come!" While we are "crying out" like this as an adult, a partner likely just hears our anger, signaling to their nervous system that there is danger here and setting off a fight-or-flight response. But again, it's perfectly normal to cry out for connection in this way.

As humans, our most fundamental, moment-to-moment question is "Are you with me?" When the answer appears to be "No" over and over again, we reach a limit. It can help us understand the validity of this response to realize that under every burst of anger is an experience of pain and fear. The baby let her sadness be known with a whimper, her fear that no one is coming with her cry, and her utter desperation because no one came with her rage. We may have more sophisticated language to express our needs as adults, but we still have the need for others to see us, to recognize our needs, and to show up for us. In our adult relationships, a healthy expression of anger might be to notice the feeling arising in us, to consult with our inner world to see what pain or fear is driving the anger, and to calmly let our partner know about the anger and where the pain or fear is coming from. This makes room for our experience without making our partner responsible for how we feel.

A lot has happened since we were the baby in the crib. The experiences that led to us being anxiously attached mean that we have a big backlog of pain and fear, so that small actions on the part of our partner can set off an avalanche of anger. But it is also more complicated than that. We have already seen that we anxious people often have a deeply rooted fear of conflict, believing that we must keep our partner happy and unchallenged in order to be loved. We believe that any sign of a rupture, particularly one we caused, could signal the end of the relationship. The thing is, emotions don't just go away if we ignore them. We may turn them against ourselves in a wave of self-criticism. And they go deeper inside, growing in intensity until the next time they are activated, like a rough finger poking a raw wound. At this point, any angry feelings that have been squashed down can become violent, aggressive, and explosive. Instead of a calm adult discussion about what's upsetting us, the feelings spill out. We might throw a tantrum and make up stories about how *they made us* feel the way we do. Instead of setting a boundary, we've ignited a firestorm. There is no blame in this. Because we didn't have the care we needed when we were young, the neural circuitry that helps us reflect on why we're angry never developed, so when the feelings get big, there is nothing to stop them from erupting. The healing path we're on now is going to remedy that so our anger can become an ally even in our closest relationships.

We learned a lot about anger in our childhood by the way the people around us experienced and expressed it. The questions below will help you gain some insight into why you deal with conflict the way you do.

How did you experience conflict in your childhood home? Was it openly expressed or hidden?

Was it safe for you to express anger? What happened when you did?

How did your parents and others handle frustration?

When people expressed their needs, did it include anger?

How do you feel about anger now? Is there a judgment around this emotion?

What messages did you learn around speaking up?

What happens inside you when you express frustration to someone you love?

How comfortable are you when anger comes up, and what do you typically do with it?

Can you see how your relationship with anger is the result of these powerful old learnings? Recognizing this is the first step to changing your patterns around anger. When we don't deal with this natural emotion, but hold it inside, we either turn it against ourselves or fall into depression—or both. The message we are giving our psyche is that there's no point in taking a stand for what we need or want, and so we shut down and simply give up. For this reason, the fight part of the fight-or-flight response that lights up our amygdala anytime our wounded Little Me feels abandoned, ignored, or misunderstood must be addressed and integrated. This begins by taking Little Me's wounds around feeling and expressing anger very seriously.

For many of us, it was scary to feel anger when we were small because expressing it brought on a threat. We might have been shouted at and told we were being bad, and to play nicely or else. Perhaps our caregiver even shut us in our room and walked away. If this was the case, did it feel safe for us to express our anger? And is it any wonder that our Little Me fears the same reaction from a partner if we express our anger with them? As we begin to ask our anger what it wants, we will start to see it as a vital part of our life force and a valuable ally in navigating our relationships.

Building our capacity to speak up when we feel angry and developing the inner balance to be able to respectfully challenge others and say no means that the appropriate expression of anger can become an aspect of our outer boundary system. This will likely require a period of trial and error, meaning we're allowed to try it out and make mistakes. But over time, we will come to value our anger for the powerful protective force that it is and see the boundaries that result from swapping people-pleasing for telling hard truths as an important part of taking care of ourselves and becoming full equal partners in our relationships.

❦

SETTING BOUNDARIES WITH MOM

Let's look at how my client Sasha learned to use her healthy anger to set boundaries in her relationships. When she came in, she told me about struggling with boundaries in just about every area of her life. Any time she got into a relationship with someone, even with friends, it felt like a lot of work. Most of all, she often found herself saying yes when she really wanted to say no, even though she felt a kind of "hot resentment" building in her chest sometimes. She was actively dating, but none of the relationships lasted beyond a few weeks. She had just about no ability to feel what she wanted or needed, so she would fade into the background, with the other person quickly losing interest in her. One of her boyfriends even told her, "You always agree with me. You never decide what we should do." She felt so ashamed, but as harsh as this was, this comment was the wake-up call she needed to come in and get some help.

After doing some digging, it was clear that Sasha grew up in a home where she was the caretaker. She was the oldest of four children and took on a lot of extra responsibilities. It was her job to keep the peace in the household because too much noise or activity made her mother anxious and her father furious. She learned, *I am lovable if I am quiet and do what others want.* When we started working on boundaries, we began with her mother, who still called her every day. She would complain for a while on the phone and Sasha would actively listen, always trying to help, while physically feeling two things: everything her mom was feeling and her own anger—which she quickly shoved away. When I asked Sasha, "Do you enjoy these calls?" she told me, "No!" The strength of her no was the first time I saw a flash of her own strong feelings.

As we listened to her Little Me, Sasha could sense how she had no room to experience her own feelings. It became clear that her anxious mother had poor boundaries with her daughter, always needing Sasha to help regulate her emotions. After a while, Sasha's anger began to make more sense to her, although it made her anxious to imagine changing her boundary around the daily calls with her mother. As we explored what that would be like, we found that Sasha's father was also part of the picture. If she wasn't able to calm her mother, he would come unglued and yell at everyone. We called on her Inner Nurturers to help Little Me feel safe with us now, so that Sasha could begin to explore setting some boundaries without Little Me's very legitimate fear welling up in an overwhelming way. We began to do some role-playing with Mom. She explained, "My first fear is what will she do if she doesn't have me to vent to? Also, what if she gets mad at me?" We began to see that these precise fears were at the root of her struggles in all her other relationships. One of the big benefits of our practice was that we were building the circuitry for Sasha to connect with her own needs and wants, including the full range of emotions she was experiencing. She was becoming more self-full.

As we continued to help Little Me with their frightening memories, Sasha realized that even if her mother *did* get mad, her body did not feel as threatened as before, even though her heart raced a bit. We followed that sensation back to Little Me's experience and held her safely again. After this practice, Sasha began to set some real boundaries with her mom and was able to return her body to a state of calm by bringing in her Inner Nurturer community and connecting to the new feelings of safety in her body.

It took time, and Sasha's mother was *not* happy at first. But Sasha persevered and felt the freedom that came from speaking up and setting limits with her mom. At one point, feeling how angry she was with her mother's daily oversharing, she strongly expressed how she didn't like the constant venting, telling her mother how it impacted her. She asked her mother to stop calling her on her lunch breaks and said that she would let her know when she had time to connect. This strong statement was a huge step. When Sasha got off this call, she was overwhelmed with anxiety. But instead of caving and calling her mother back, she stayed with the discomfort and allowed it to settle. This "gap" in communication is another example of a healthy boundary and is the result of Sasha building her inner team to help her regulate. Two days later, Sasha's mother called her and shared that she could see how her daily complaints had been hurting her daughter and actually apologized. Sasha could hardly believe this. In this interaction, Sasha had an experience that it could be safe to not leap in to fix her own anxiety by apologizing, removing the boundary she had set, and subjugating her needs once again.

Over time, Sasha started dating again, and told me that she felt sexier and more empowered when she was able to speak her own mind. Little by little, she learned that not only was it okay to express her truth, but that this led to healthier, more balanced relationships. She also discovered that asking for her needs to be met did not take away from her ability to show up for others. It simply helped her to attract partners who mirrored the newfound respect she was able to show herself.

WHEN VULNERABILITY LEADS TO INTIMACY

As we can see from Sasha's story, as much as setting a boundary is about self-protection, it also makes us vulnerable to rejection. Given that anxious people have a deep-seated fear of abandonment, it is so hard for us to say "no," or to voice any needs that we feel may push a partner away. It's scary to ask for what we need—especially love—when we fear we may not get it. But the only way to true intimacy is to feel the fear of rejection, spend time helping Little Me with their core wounds, and have the courage to ask for what we need anyway.

Giving ourselves permission to speak up in this way can take practice. Over time, it will help us develop a boundary system that suits who we are. For example, introverts often have different kinds of boundaries than extroverts. Because introverts spend so much time in their own inner world, they are able to reflect on what kind of boundaries would feel good and right to them, but it may take a while to tell their partner. Extroverts tend to figure out what they want and need from interactions with others, so they may come up with boundaries on the spot and express them quickly and directly. Matching our boundary-setting to our emerging self-full sense of who we are is an ongoing process. As our healing progresses, our boundaries will also continue to shift, becoming both more clear and more fluidly responsive to current conditions. When there is less to protect inside, there is more room to express our authentic feelings with those who are dear to us.

In the process, we will also be letting go of the need to manage our partner's emotions. If we are allowed to feel what we feel, so are they. Any time we start hiding our true selves out of fear of how others may respond, not only are we on the path to abandoning ourselves, we are shutting down the opportunity to learn from each other and potentially grow closer. In the midst of our healing process, we can feel the tug-of-war between our fear of losing someone and the joy of beginning to sense the power of clear boundaries. Becoming more self-full, we begin to sense the importance of both kinds of boundaries—those that let us say "yes" to our own needs and those that allow us to say "no" to the needs of others.

If we're in a relationship where our partner shuts us down anytime we challenge them or express a need, this person will never have the chance to meet our whole self. In healthy relationships, people allow each other to make requests and set limits, and are then open to hearing how that response affects the other person. This can become a powerful cycle of growth for both people. In every case, this begins with us knowing what we need, something that emerges in the course of healing, and understanding that there is no shame or acute danger in expressing this. If you find yourself struggling with setting a boundary out of fear of conflict or rejection, it's an invitation to spend time with Little Me. You can work with the exercise in the next section to practice setting limits in a healthy way.

OWN YOUR SOVEREIGN "NO"

Step 1: Pressing Pause

Because we want to keep people happy, our first response when facing a request may be to say "yes" even if it means putting our own needs aside to offer far beyond what we can realistically provide. What we need is to buy ourselves time to think things through so we can respond in a way that is more in tune with our desires and our capacity. No matter what knee-jerk response arises in you, if you're unsure, say, "I don't know. I need to get back to you."

Step 2: Dialoguing with Our Inner World

Once we have stepped away from the situation, we can check in with our Little Me parts about what response is in our highest good, including the good of the relationship. We can close our eyes and visit these Little Me aspects in our Safe Place. We can ask them what they want and if anything is upsetting them. We can call on our Inner Nurturers to help us listen to our Little Me parts. The first step here is listening to whether Little Me would say "yes" or "no" based on their needs and wants rather than on concern about how the other person will respond. Would Little Me feel joy in doing this? Do they feel they can give what is asked without abandoning themselves? When they begin to worry about the other person's reaction, we can let Little Me know that we'll be with that after we make the decision about what to do.

Step 3: Is It a "Yes" or a "No"?

As we take the time to check in with our Little Mes, we will often begin to feel a natural "yes" or a "no" in our bodies. We can try on both responses to see how our bellies, our muscles, and our hearts respond to each. With which response does our belly soften, our heart expand, and our muscles relax? Sometimes the answer is immediately clear, sometimes not. Take all the time you need as this kind of listening is a newly developing skill. You are now entering a space where you can listen to the wisdom of your body. The more you practice, the more you will feel the energy of your sovereign "yes" and "no" responses.

Step 4: Moving from Feeling the Sovereign "No" to Acting on the Sovereign "No"

If the answer is "yes," it's easy to move ahead. But when the "no" comes, our feelings about acting on this "no" may become strong. It is no longer a hypothetical but something we are actually going to do. We can return to Little Me and our Inner Nurturers as we visualize offering our "no." We can let them know that it's natural to be concerned about other people's reactions or to feel guilt around saying no and then explore the why behind these feelings. Perhaps Little Me is scared they will be abandoned, or maybe their Inner Protectors want to hustle them into doing something because it will "look good." We can listen to everything Little Me has to say.

Step 4: Communicating Our Boundary Clearly

When we're clear about what we actually want to express and the emotional response to the request in our body is calming, we are ready to return to the situation and communicate our boundary with a calm, adult voice. Perhaps it's a "no," or maybe it's a "yes" with some conditions and limits attached. Because of the inner work we've been doing, we will feel less need to follow the fear-based urge to explain ourselves or to apologize for our response. Respecting ourselves and our needs and limits in this way will help the other person respect the boundary we are setting. This will increase the safety and the intimacy between you.

❤❤

WHEN A WALL BECOMES A GATE

Is there a time when setting a boundary means closing the door on a relationship and throwing away the key? Yes, sometimes two people's needs are so incompatible that intimate relationship isn't possible. We'll talk more about this in the next section. Often, even a hard line in the sand can have a little room for flexibility. For example, if your partner can't stop engaging in a behavior that upsets you, the self-full option (and another kind of boundary) might be to choose to accept this person as they are and decide how to give yourself what you need in order to move forward. That outcome could look very different depending on your individual circumstances.

For example, if your partner feels the need to work one day on the weekend after you two had agreed that weekends were permanently off-limits for business, you might begin by having to sit with the disappointment. Is it touching Little Me and reminding them of previous times when promises went unkept? If you find this to be true, is it possible to take some time with Little Me before making a relationship-altering decision? Do you notice an easing of feelings and possibly the emergence of other alternatives than breaking up as Little Me feels heard and cared for? Are there any compromises to be made? When you begin to think this way, it is often a sign that your adult self is returning to the forefront. Now might be the time to talk with your partner to see if she or he has any ideas about what to do with this impasse. If it still seems like weekend work is going to become the norm, you can then decide if you want to do something creative with this time on your own. One of my clients decided to get a master's degree in creative writing when her partner got engulfed in work. A lot depends on the quality of the relationship overall. My client felt that there was far more satisfaction and care in this relationship than any she had experienced. Her adult self decided that, on balance, it was good to stay. No relationship is perfect. Some decisions and behaviors we learn to accommodate, while others will lead to us drawing a firmer line.

As with everything, the boundaries we set from a place of self-fullness exist on a spectrum. There are the small daily ways we can check in with ourselves and see what we need without making a specific request, just to be sure we're staying aware of our needs and preferences. There is standing up for ourselves, being vulnerable, and asking to have these needs met. There is removing ourselves from a situation until we're in the right space to say yes or no to a request. There are moments when respectful anger is needed to make ourselves clear. And there is showing our partner the door. At the extreme end of the boundary spectrum, rigid walls that can turn a relationship into a prison may go up. They also stem from fear—not of abandonment but of invasion and enmeshment. People with anxious attachment are less likely to erect these barriers but certainly may feel them from our avoidantly attached partners. Our quest is to become self-full so we can be sensitive *and* strong, which gives us room to build some flexibility into our boundary system. Let me show you how this works.

Imagine that your body, mind, heart, and spirit are your home. When you keep your home well maintained, you feel safe inside it, and you're motivated to make it somewhere you want to spend time. Now imagine your wider energy system is like a fence surrounding your property. It has a gate so you can decide whom to let in. When you meet someone new, you might not invite them into your home right away. You'll likely spend some time getting to know this person first. Once you've built some trust, you may issue a dinner invitation. Eventually, they may even stay the night. But all of this has happened over time, as you have had more experience and gotten used to letting someone into your physical, emotional, and spiritual space. At the same time, trust also allows you to be comfortable with this person leaving and coming back.

This analogy represents the natural ebb and flow in an interdependent relationship that develops as we invite somebody to share in our intimate world. Perhaps you can sense the importance of having enough distance to be able to come back to yourself and tend to your own inner space. In a boundaryless situation, this new person would have stayed over the first time you met and moved all his or her stuff in the very next day, cluttering up the hallways and filling your home with noise and mess.

This second scenario is not uncommon among anxious people whose early life experience has explicitly undermined their ability to sense where their personal property line ends. When this is combined with the fear that they are unlovable, they might let just anyone in, because the offer may never come again. Simply having another warm body in their home helps them feel less alone. Sometimes it goes the other way and they are too afraid to let anyone into this home at first. But once they let another person in and attach, they are very unlikely to ever escort them out if needed. Both of these paths bypass the natural progression toward true intimacy. It also shows that their Little Me is so frightened of abandonment that it is very difficult to manage the transitions between connection and separation that are a natural and important part of any relationship.

When this is the case, it might feel so good when someone enters your home, you never want this person to leave. Deep down, you fear that they will walk out the door and never come back. Now you are willing to bend over backward to get this individual to stay, replacing all the food in the refrigerator with things they like to eat, cleaning up after this person, and even redecorating the place. When this doesn't work and they decide to leave anyway (even if it's just to go to the store), you might pack up your bags and abandon your own home to go with them. If your early wounds are deep enough, you may not even notice that you have become homeless until the other person, perhaps feeling your desperation, leaves.

One of the most valuable lessons here is that the better we get about maintaining our boundaries, the more we are able to respect other people's need for space, too. The same way somebody we just met would get freaked out if we invited him or her over and didn't let them leave, we would feel equally distressed if they showed up with a suitcase and announced they were moving in. This is how it can feel when people who are anxiously attached decide that their new crushes are "the one" and start doing anything they can to keep them by their side. Everybody needs space, and when you understand this about yourself, your partner's need to separate from time to time begins to feel less like abandonment and more like a healthy breather to replenish and reestablish his or her own sense of self.

If the "home" analogy works for you, you can return to it as you learn to listen to the bodily sensations that are part of your boundary system. When does it feel like your home is being invaded? When does it feel safe to let somebody in? And when do you need some alone time to tidy up, rest, and reset? Perhaps you can even create an Inner Safe Place in this home to dialogue with your Little Me and your Inner Nurturers, seeing these conversations as part of the regular maintenance that will make your inner world a daily welcoming haven for you. Over time, protecting this space by practicing discernment around who and what you allow in will start to become second nature.

KNOW YOUR NON-NEGOTIABLES

While flexible boundaries are an essential part of developing a stable sense of connection with a partner, it's equally important to know our relationship non-negotiables. While we experience many of these behaviors as essential (such as responsible spending habits) or completely off-limits (like smoking or cheating), they can also include religious orientation, political alignment, dedication to various causes, and more. It's important to identify these for ourselves. We can start with being clear about physical violence and other extreme violations of the self, but from there, the matter becomes strictly personal.

Making some lists could help you begin to identify areas where no compromise is possible without abandoning your self, areas where compromise seems possible, and areas where there is simply no challenge. On a piece of paper, make three columns labeled "No Way," "Maybe," and "Yes!" Then ask yourself this question about any areas that come to mind.

If my partner [fill in an activity, a preference, a behavior], I can't be with them/I can tolerate it/I wouldn't mind at all.

A friend of mine did this exercise with me and found that her non-negotiables quickly emerged simply because she had asked the question. No smoking, no cheating, no racist leanings, no children, no previous marriages, must have a spiritual life, no daily drinking, must want kids. In the process, she also discovered some areas that really lit her up! Having different spiritual interests, liking different kinds of music, loving to travel, and more. It helped her get in touch with the adventurer and curious seeker in her. She also found some areas where compromise would be possible, such as where they might live and how many kids to have. Even though she had preferences, they didn't feel set in stone.

Our work with Little Me is helping us get in touch with what really matters to us. Without a sense of our true selves, non-negotiables are hard to spot, so we can walk into relationships that are too painful to endure. It's also true that both people mostly put their best foot forward at the beginning of a relationship, and increasing intimacy will reveal sides we didn't know were there. Once we have discovered this and have a clear sense of our non-negotiables, the best boundary is often to simply walk away. My client Rebecca is a great example of this.

Standing Strong for What Matters Most

Rebecca had been dating Mike for four years. As she began to describe their relationship to me, she shared that he had originally been attentive, but now was busy most of the week, and would drink Saturday away after playing tennis with his buddies. As a result, she only got to be with him on Sunday, when she would spend most of the day trying to get his attention while he nursed a hangover. Rebecca had been in several abusive relationships and stressed that Mike was not controlling or abusive toward her, but that equally he was not showing any signs of wanting to move the relationship forward. She felt like she was last on his list, and his actions seemed to prove this.

Meanwhile, Rebecca badly wanted to start a family and create a life with someone who wanted to share in that experience. They had talked about this early in their relationship with Mike expressing that this was what he wanted, too. She and Mike lived together in the apartment she owned and where she took on all the domestic responsibilities. Resentment began to build over time, but not to the point that she was considering leaving until one day he commented: "I don't think I ever want to have children. If we both work really hard and stay in this apartment, we can retire early and have an easy life." Not only did her blood begin to boil, she also felt as if her dreams were being shattered. She knew she had to do something.

Getting more in touch with her Little Me and strong community of Inner Nurturers that included a compassionate grandmother, Rebecca began to see that Mike had actually been showing up as Mike for a long time. He might have told her he wanted the same things as she did, but his actions never lined up. For her part, Rebecca had been ignoring all the signs and remaining attached to the possibility of what could be out of fear of being alone again and having to start over. As we deepened in our healing work, she became more able to acknowledge that she felt deeply hurt and misunderstood, and decided it was time for her to make her own needs a priority.

While she knew she was risking losing him, Rebecca finally mustered the courage to tell Mike what she needed. Even the thought of this brought on anxiety, but she called on her inner team to be with her during this brave move. She reminded her Little Me that she was worthy of having a partner who wanted the same things she did. Eventually, she got up the courage to tell Mike that if he truly did not want a family, they would have to break up.

He was adamant about not wanting any children, and Rebecca left the relationship soon after that. Rebecca shared with me how this experience had been for her. As well as reaching out for support from her friends, she told me that she'd been able to ride out the waves of loneliness she sometimes felt at night with the help of both her Inner Nurturers and her little dog. Knowing that the dog was there next to her helped her feel less alone, and she had her community of Nurturers to soothe her frightened Little Me by reminding her that the relationship with Mike was never going to bring her what she needed. Because she had the support she needed, she was able to move through this period of separation in a way that was actually healing for her.

Rebecca's story is a perfect example of setting a hard boundary from a self-full place. It also shows that ending a relationship does not mean being alone. Rebecca knew she needed the support of reliable friends, her therapist, and her dog to help her through the transition of her breakup, not to medicate her feelings of loneliness, but to remind herself that she was worthy of healthy, secure connections. Four-legged friends are wonderful for this as they offer unconditional love, something I came to value myself when I was learning to become self-full following my divorce. My little dog Tito (R.I.P.) was always there for me, no matter what, which became an external reminder of how secure attachment feels. He was preparing me for a secure relationship with another human being one day.

THE ULTIMATE BOUNDARY: LEARNING TO LET GO

The other vital lesson Rebecca learned from her relationship with Mike was the possibility of letting go. When we consider that connection is a biological imperative, letting go is going to be challenging for most of us, although those of us who are anxiously attached get a double dose as our childhood wounds are activated. In Rebecca's case, she clung to the fantasy of who she wanted Mike to be for four whole years. But staying in a relationship out of fear of being alone or because we're convinced that it's as good as we'll get is blocking us from the love and the relationship that we truly need and deserve.

Sometimes instigating a breakup, like Rebecca did, is only the first step to truly letting go. If part of us remains attached to the fantasy of the relationship, or if we "keep the fires burning" by staying in contact with the other person because it feels too vulnerable to close the door completely, this person will stay in our energy field, weighing us down and preventing us from fully moving on. This also makes us more vulnerable to what's called *hoovering*, a modern term for when an ex keeps trying to come back into our life, as they "suck" us toward reconnecting. The only way to prevent this is to release any old attachments once and for all, which means fully grieving the lost dream while putting boundaries in place that stop contact.

It isn't only our Little Me who feels the pain of letting go, but our adult self who invested wholeheartedly in this relationship. Along with heartbroken tears, denial, bargaining, and anger are also part of a thorough grieving process. Having someone—or several someones—who can support us while we are thrown around by these emotions will give us the safety to do it well. It is cleansing for every part of us—body, mind, heart, and spirit—to grieve in this way. Instead of blocking our emotions by holding on to even small pieces of the relationship, it's more healing to step into this grief and work with it to give us the freedom to keep loving deeply with a big, open heart.

Often, grieving the end of a relationship takes time and happens in layers. We anxious people have a tendency to let go a little slower as we move through the process of grief because we attach so deeply, and transitioning back to ourselves can be a daunting experience. It is especially important for us to lean on positive external support as we move into this process. It is actually healthy and normal to reach out. By leaning on friends and family who just listen to us, we can slowly peel back the layers of grief while filling in the gaps with people who can offer us love and support. Author and psychotherapist Dr. Sue Johnson points out in her book *Hold Me Tight*, "Suffering is a given; suffering alone is intolerable."

I often hear people say, "The relationship wasn't great, but I still really miss him." Regardless of the quality of the relationship, a loss is still a loss. This is likely a familiar experience for Little Me, so it's normal for the little ones inside to want to hang on to the good times. Outer support coupled with the kind presence of our Inner Nurturers can help us remember that these feelings of loss are real and that they will also pass. Whenever we grieve a current loss, earlier times of abandonment and aloneness rise to the surface. When we understand this, we can be compassionate with ourselves as we move slowly through the process of letting go. These can be times of even deeper healing, preparing us for a healthier partnership in the future.

Coming out on the other side with some support, we will find ourselves more able to stay open to connection, while being okay with being apart. We will know more clearly what we need, and that it's okay to ask for this. We'll be less tempted to control others and more able to adapt our own behaviors to better care for our selves. Above all, it means respecting our own relationship non-negotiables and being willing to let go completely when a hard boundary has been crossed.

Ultimately, this is the only way to create space for our own growth and to deepen our connections with the people who are offering healthy and fulfilling attachments. Are you still questioning whether this will ever be possible for you? As you are about to discover, all the work we are doing together is preparing you to create the safety and stability you crave in your relationships. In the next chapter, we will explore a new way to love and be loved, which is about what we can bring into a relationship rather than looking for a partner to complete us.

CHAPTER 8

A New Way to Love and Be Loved

There's no such thing as a "perfect" relationship because there is no such thing as a "perfect" human being. We all have our wounds and our unique ways of expressing and compensating for them, and our relationships with one another are often where these wounds are awakened. The work we have been doing in this book—the work of being self-full—is essentially a process for healing childhood wounds by developing a strong relationship with our Inner Nurturers, those voices within us that hold the presence of those who have loved and supported us throughout our lives. When we talk about self-nurturing, this is what is really happening within us. With these inner relationships established, we have been working to mend our core wounds and reshape our neural circuits for security. The relationship you and I have developed as we've journeyed together through this book is part of this process. I want you to know that this ongoing companionship will always be with you.

Let's pause for a moment and consider what a lovely thing it is that our brains can be rewired so that we feel much more settled and safe in our relationships, regardless of our age and regardless of the depth of our earlier wounding. In this process, our ANS is being soothed so it can more easily find calm when we feel anxiety arise. Our reactions are also slowing down, so we can have big feelings without lashing out or grasping for others to fix them. We are more able to connect with our own needs and wants, and move into relationships with the intention of balancing our needs with those of our partners. Our capacity for empathy is expanding, so our partners will feel seen and known by us as well. Because of all this, our intimate connections are becoming a place to heal and grow together rather than just the means to soothe our constant anxiety. This work is ongoing. Our current and future relationships are where we practice relating differently. While I can't promise the fantasy happily-ever-after ending you have been fed since you were little, you will discover that through this inner work you have actually been experiencing a whole new way to love and be loved. This will have a profound impact on both how you show up in relationships and the kind of partners you attract.

As you continue to feel seen and valued by those who support you, your self-worth will grow. You will naturally begin to align with others—including friends and colleagues—who value you in this way, too. You will be much less likely to unconsciously seek out unavailable partners whose behaviors seem to validate the false idea that you are inherently unlovable. If you are in a relationship already, the changes happening inside you will also affect your partner in unpredictable ways. As we have seen, one person thriving and developing a stronger sense of self does not necessarily lead to similar changes in another. Our greater availability for intimacy can frighten partners who have adapted to their own pain by becoming avoidant. Our growing compassion for what is bringing on this avoidance may be enough for our partners to want to seek their healing, too. Or the wounds may simply run too deep and the relationship will find its end. Even when the relationship lasts, it doesn't mean it's going to be all roses from here on in. Conflict in relationships is inevitable, and part of becoming more self-full also means leaning into these natural "ruptures," which can even deepen our awareness of each other's needs when approached as an opportunity to grow. Every rupture that is followed by a repair actually strengthens our connection with other people.

Your ability to press pause on your emotional reactions is a strong ally because it gives you time to communicate what's going on inside in ways that will actually help you get your needs met rather than adding more fuel to the fire by reacting with anger or blame. As our healing deepens, we become more sensitive to the tender spots in our Little Me and more open to hearing about those same places in our partner. No matter how much healing we do, our relationships will always bring up more for us to become aware of as we engage in the beautiful dance of interdependence. Rather than making our struggles all about our partner, we are learning to take ownership of any pain and fear that's been hiding out in the dusty, forgotten corners of our anxious attachment system. All the work we are doing together has been leading you here. In this chapter, we're going to apply what you are learning—and even more important, what you are experiencing— to the way you relate to others, regardless of your current relationship status.

WHEN THE HONEYMOON (PHASE) IS OVER

As a couples therapist, I get so upset with the way our culture glorifies romantic love, setting up expectations for this to be a constant portal of bliss when that just isn't the case. In reality, the relationship only begins *after* the dopamine-fueled honeymoon phase has run its course, when the rose-tinted spectacles come off and we are able to see our partners for who they really are, flaws and all. This phase unfolds differently for each couple, but there are certain hallmarks we can count on. It is a time of deepening in which both individuals begin to show more sides of themselves. Both of their Little Mes can become activated by this. An avoidant person may step back in the relationship a bit and spend more time at work. This may agitate an anxious Little Me who has fears of abandonment. And so the stage is set for the familiar childhood dance that has remained out of sight until now. Other patterns can happen as well. Two avoidant people may begin to return to their individual lives and wonder where the passion went as they walk parallel paths rather than find interdependence. Two anxious people may continue to cling in ways that fuel the drama. But when one or both partners are capable of secure attachment, this can be a rich time of discovery, and creative compromises may emerge that become the building blocks of a truly fulfilling interdependent partnership.

In any case, this period will bring its challenges. It is scary to find that our perfect lover can also be demanding or whiny or stubborn, or insists on cooking food we can't stand. And when we're afraid, one of our go-to responses can be anger. Now we can begin to feel like we're locked in a power struggle as we negotiate our individual needs in this relationship. One partner might say he needs a night out with friends once a week. The other might insist that wine at dinner is important to her. Issues large and small will inevitably involve a series of requests that call for compromises. When those needs hit a sore spot or a non-negotiable in the other person, this can be a time of rupture, leading to arguments and disagreements. It's also when a relationship can begin to feel like "work," and we may find ourselves questioning whether it's worth it.

Not only is this very normal, it is also part of a healthy process of defining our boundaries in the relationship. At the same time, we are learning more about who our partner is, and that certainly has the potential of deepening the connection. When couples say they "never fight," I always suspect that one person is doing the majority of the compromising (by being selfless). At the other end of the spectrum, there may be near-constant fighting because the two people have incompatible non-negotiables and so are consistently walking over each other's basic needs. At this point, the self-full thing might be to end the relationship. But when two people find they are compatible in the areas that matter most, are willing to keep talking and finding compromises, have a basic respect for each other's needs, and desire commitment even when the "love drugs" have worn off, they are on the way to something special.

I've seen the honeymoon phase last from a few days, to weeks, months, and even a couple of years. As the chemical rush decreases, each of you gets to decide whether there is enough good stuff to dare to peek under the hood. Two questions may come up at this point: Is it possible this relationship will satisfy my need for deepening connection? Is this person also interested in our relationship becoming a place in which we can both grow? It takes time to get clear answers on both of these, but with patience and a willingness to get vulnerable and have hard conversations, clarity will come. We may also notice that none of this fits with our image of the dream relationship. Given how easy it is to pull up a dating app and find somebody new for the next "honeymoon," it's also when many of us jump ship. But if we back off when the going gets tough, we are walking away from an opportunity for exponential personal growth, something that will impact all of our relationships, including with friends, family, and colleagues, and not least in our relationship with our wounded Little Me.

Given society's unrealistic expectations for love, navigating conflict is always going to be challenging. For those of us who are anxiously attached, the first sign of a rupture can send us spiraling back into old patterns of selflessness and codependency. Even though we have been working with Little Me, being in the trenches with another live human being is a whole different challenge. When the old abandonment wound kicks in, we may reach out or lash out in a desperate attempt to get the love and attention we crave. Realizing we are no longer in total sync with our lover, this person who made us feel so seen by the way they seemed so perfectly attuned to our needs, Little Me can even feel betrayed. This is an important place to pause and turn to our supportive people while we go back to the practices in chapters 5 and 6, before this new relationship devolves into an endless debate over who's the "bad guy," the selfish narcissist or the clingy child. We tend to see in black and white when we are lost in our wounds, but as our Little Me connects again with our Inner Nurturers, our system will calm down and we will see that nobody is to blame for what's come up. We will begin to sense that any pain and fear we are feeling has not necessarily been caused by our partner; rather, it's likely he or she has stepped on a land mine deep inside us, unaware of the wounding that lies beneath.

Once we have our inner bearings, we can also more easily re-member that these ruptures are actually a normal part of forming healthy, secure attachments. It turns out we humans are all quite fallible, even on a good day! Research on well-attached mothers and their babies shows that more than half of their interactions can be out of sync, and that what matters is that they are able to repair these moments of dysregulation to come back into connection. Our caregivers generally do the best they can to attune to us, and when for whatever reason they are unable to do this, showing us their *intention* to repair our distress is an extremely important part of the process of developing secure attachment. In practice, this might look like them acknowledging our distress, asking what is wrong, and validating how we feel. This deceptively simple interaction teaches our nervous system that they did not intentionally hurt or abandon us, and that, eventually, we will have the opportunity to get our needs met. A very big part of the repair is simply to feel seen and heard, before we even get to a solution to the actual problem.

Stability and longevity in relationships is built on mutual respect, transparency, vulnerability, humility, and the capacity to deeply listen to our partner. These qualities create the safety that is necessary to repair ruptures when things get turbulent. Rather than assigning blame, this means developing empathy for the fact that each person has very different needs and perspectives in some areas, and that's okay. Each person also has a history that is guiding how each responds under stress. As we become more familiar with how our wounds shape our responses, we can become curious about that same process in our partner, particularly when the responses we are getting feel defensive. All people—including us—respond in mean and blaming ways when they are frightened and need to protect themselves. When those responses are met with curiosity rather than judgment or fighting back, there's a good possibility that it will be safe enough to talk more honestly about what is happening. Ultimately, resolution begins by honoring whatever is present and giving each person full permission to share, while staying open and curious about the outcome. We have been practicing this internally within our own inner community and on the outside in relationships that are generally less high stakes than a romance. So now it is time to stretch and offer these gifts to our partner.

As you continue to heal, you are more likely to attract partners with a similar capacity for working to create secure attachment. But rather than your old anxious tendencies going away, they will also continue to show up in secure relationships, the difference being that now you are developing the ability to see what is happening and approach things differently. For any relationship to work out in the long run, however, it's important that you are *both* committed to looking deeper when issues arise. This is what makes it safe for the relationship *not* to be perfect. Instead, when you're both realistic about the work involved in truly getting to know (and love) each other, having your "stuff" come up becomes an opportunity for ever-deepening intimacy. This means having the capacity to acknowledge the old patterns that are firing. It means reacting less often, and instead pressing pause together so that you can take the time to really hear what's actually going on for each of you. Harville Hendrix, the cofounder of Imago Relationship Therapy, refers to this as "conscious partnership." The honeymoon may be over, but your love will be deeper and more satisfying than anything you experienced in the heat of the initial romantic attraction. As more parts of you both are received with care, safety will deepen, leading to more vulnerability and intimacy. You're becoming closer each day.

WHOSE TRUTH IS IT, ANYWAY?

Not that it feels that way at first. It may not surprise you to hear that ninety-nine percent of the time couples come into my office ready for World War III. Often, they feel as if they are speaking to a brick wall and want me to make their partner see "what's really going on." But healing in relationships doesn't come from trying to prove our point. It's actually the opposite that needs to happen. Instead of focusing on winning the argument and making the other person see things our way, we have to remember we are both on the same team, and that both our viewpoints make sense from our own perspectives. No feeling is ever wrong, and even facts take on different meanings for people. When our emotions are running strong, it can be hard to remember what's even been said.

In my office, I often use my cell phone to illustrate this. I have couples sit across from each other and I hold my phone up in the middle. One of them is looking at the front screen, which usually has a picture of my dog, while the other person looks at the back of the phone, at the camera lens and case. Then I ask them to tell me what my phone looks like. Of course, they each share something very different, even though they are in fact describing the same thing. Then we stop so I can explain that this is where all couples get stuck, endlessly arguing about what they see and feel is the truth, when in fact there are always many different ways of seeing things depending on each person's perspective.

We talk about how empathy arises when we stop trying to prove that our viewpoint is right and instead get curious about seeing things through our partner's lens. Often, I ask them to each put aside what they saw on my phone and instead imagine seeing it (literally) from where the other person is sitting. Same phone, different view. No one is wrong in this scenario, and there is no need to fight it out. This simple exercise helps couples understand that trying to determine what really happened is less important than their willingness to honor that each person's experience is real *for them*. The next step is to commit to discovering just which lenses come into play in our disagreements. This begins as work with Little Me for both individuals, which means connecting with core wounds.

Side by side with this, it may mean examining which potent cultural messages may have shaped us. When each person in the couple can share their childhood experiences of relationships, whether in the family or what society led them to expect, it is quite natural for the listening partner to feel empathy for the pain and fear that shaped the responses that come most naturally now. This work is the bedrock of mature, interdependent relationships. With practice, when disagreements come up, judgments and arguments are replaced by openness and empathy. Voices will soften, ruptures will be repaired, and both people will be healing and growing together. The relationship will be consistently steered from Me versus You toward becoming Team Us.

That last paragraph is an outline that gives us the sense of what is possible. As we step into it, we'll find it's a messier process. All of us have developed protections—avoidance, anger, blaming, hiding, caretaking, to name just a few—that have become deeply ingrained over time. They are guarding Little Me's wounds and so they are valuable allies. But, as indestructible as they may feel, they will give way of their own accord as soon as there is more healing and safety in the relationship. This takes time, however, and there will be a lot of back-and-forth while we're in the thick of it. One day, both partners are feeling stable enough to be curious and caring when one brings up a sore topic. Another day, one or both are tired or getting sick or the topic is too tender, and they will fall back into the old protections. Maybe there'll be a fight, ending with both partners sleeping in separate beds. But when both have agreed to be in this healing process together, they can pick up where they left off the next day with compassion for where things got derailed.

But if we know this, why can't we just make a decision to be different? As we have learned, we begin to form expectations of what our relationships will be like in infancy. Part of this is recorded in our ANS. If our parents aren't able to provide warm, safe connection a good part of the time, our sympathetic fight-or-flight response is on a lot. We begin to anticipate that our closest people won't come to help us when we feel disconnected, and so we begin to alter our behaviors to keep them as close to us as we can. As we get older, we begin to try to "make sense" of what's happening in our body and emotions by turning feelings into beliefs about our lack of value, our parents' disinterest in us, what we can expect from others, and what we have to do to keep people with us. At the same time, we also develop a set of protections to keep people from hurting us more. This is where judgment, blame, and the need to be right come in. By the time we're adults, we've practiced these so many times that they've become part of who we are. Their job is to come to our aid automatically anytime our sensitive Little Me is awakened, especially in our closest relationships.

With our most intimate connections, the way we adapted by learning to detect subtle shifts in our parents' attitudes or behaviors comes into play. A forgotten text or a throwaway comment can be enough to set off a train of thoughts that aligns with our deepest fears and reinforces the beliefs behind them. Our nervous system is unconsciously scanning for familiar kinds of danger so that our well-developed protections can leap in to save us. It's as automatic as the way we drive our car without thinking about it. Because the emotions and sensations in the old wounds that are awakening *feel* like they are happening right now, our mind searches around for a story to explain what's going on in our current relationship. Building on the small things that have gone wrong, we put together a case for why we feel so anxious and how it is our partner's fault. We are now primed to gather yet more evidence that our partner doesn't love us and will surely soon abandon us. This is all a form of self-protection, based on ancient conditioning that developed to keep our Little Me safe. Sadly, clinging to our story about what's going on only creates a barrier to us actually asking for, and receiving, what we need. At the same time, we feel too unsafe to get curious about how our partner may be hurting, too.

The key to keeping a curious, open mind instead of leaping to conclusions and imagining worst-case scenarios, which in turn makes them more likely to come true, lies in being able to slow down and stay connected to what may be happening for both people. Fear adaptively makes us focus on the thing that is frightening us, while calm allows us to see the bigger picture. The work we're doing with Little Me in this book is gradually building the neural connections for us to be able to do this. We might first notice that our anxiety is rising and decide to call a trusted friend or spend time with our Inner Nurturers. As we get a little calmer, we are more likely to be able to put whichever of our partner's actions scared us into context. For example, we might remember that our partner is going through a busy and stressful period at work and has less time to respond to texts right now. Feeling more ease, we can remember that the depth of connection in all relationships ebbs and flows, depending on what's happening for each partner outside of the relational space. We might even remember a recent time when we didn't have the bandwidth to listen to our beloved when he or she asked for some time to talk through a dilemma. Now, instead of complaining about the lack of contact during the day, we may be more able to meet our lover at the door with empathy and ask how the day has gone.

Things can go the other way, too. When your partner comes home and the first thing he says is "Where were you when I called today?" the accusatory tone, more than the words, immediately brings up the urge to defend and protect yourself. If you can keep your partner's core wounds in mind, you may be able to hear the fear beneath the snarkiness. You remember that, as a child, his mother repeatedly didn't pick him up at school because she was too drunk to drive. Because of the sharing the two of you have done, you feel sadness for that scared, abandoned child and wonder if that is why you not answering your phone is this big of a deal. Maybe the first thing you say is "I'm sorry I scared you," responding to the big picture of what you know about him rather than the angry Protector who called you out. If you two have been practicing this deeper kind of seeing for a while, your gentle words make him feel safe enough to say, "I'm sorry I snapped at you." When we see each other's Little Me as always being part of the conversation, we can sometimes let go of our knee-jerk protective response to allow for healing and deepening of intimacy to happen.

Early in the process in couples therapy, what I often see when two partners reach a point of rupture in a relationship is a domino effect where one person goes into protection mode, setting off an equal and opposite reaction in his or her partner. What's needed at that point is the support of another person, in this case me, to help slow things down and to model a different response. My curiosity about what is hurting or scaring each of them gradually becomes a new way for them to see each other. In this scenario, I become part of their Inner Nurturers' voices and way of seeing. Being with each person's core wounds in a tender, safe way helps each of their Little Mes become part of how they see and understand each other.

In chapters 5 and 6, we engaged with just this kind of work. Sharing this book with your partner, if he or she is willing, can help both of you have exactly the same kind of conversations you would have in my office. This will put you both in a much better position to risk getting vulnerable in openly sharing what you need—without blaming each other for how you feel. Perhaps you need more attention, or maybe it's simply the reassurance that you are loved. Developing the ability to have honest, compassionate conversations, even when you are in pain, is a vital part of becoming self-full and creating lasting intimacy and interdependence.

STRETCHING TO FORM CONNECTION

In times of heightened distress, we experience a sort of "contraction" as our old pains and fears wake up and narrow our focus and attention on the feeling of not being safe. As we are creating a healthier relationship, the opposite needs to happen. Both people must be willing to stretch outside their comfort zones and try out new ways of responding when they are feeling upset.

When we talked about boundaries, we saw that people with different temperaments and histories have their individual ways of setting them. The same is true for protections. When the fear of abandonment is set off, anxious people often leap to try to resolve things right away. The increased anxiety of uncertainty torments them: They need answers, they need a resolution, and they need them now! Their emotions are overwhelming and expand in all directions, causing them to reach out like the many limbs of an octopus in an attempt to find something stable to grab hold of. If they aren't met with the amount of reassurance they need, they may escalate into rage, forcing conflict in order to continue the contact and perhaps get what they need. This might look like criticizing, blaming, name-calling, screaming, or even throwing things. If this pattern worked in childhood, or if they saw their parents fight this way, it is already wired in and ready to go.

Avoidant people generally approach danger differently. For one thing, what feels dangerous to them is *more* intimacy, not less. While they are generally unaware of it, their systems are filled with the pain of not being emotionally cared for when young, so it is threatening for someone to ask them to soften and come in closer. Their response to fear may be to shut down and "turtle in." They can look quite reasonable, finding all kinds of logical explanations to not get closer, but inside there is a deep mistrust of vulnerability and what it could bring. Under greater pressure, they may get angry, sarcastic, or demeaning in an effort to shame their partner into retreating for the moment or going away completely. It is likely that everyone in their family responded to emotional needs this way, so again, the responses are deeply wired in.

Every couple's actual patterns will be different, but you get the idea of how quickly and deeply people pull apart from each other when they are in warring camps. Here's the good news. The biggest growth spot when it comes to learning a new way to love and be loved can be found in these moments of meltdown and mutual rupture. In the height of these emotional entanglements, everything we need to start down a new path is in the room—two Little Mes who are scared, two people who want to connect, two brains that can be rewired to respond differently, and two partners with the potential to transform their relationship into a sanctuary. This is where those love muscles need stretching.

For people who tend to shut down when they're in pain and who cope by holding their emotions in, it can be very hard work to learn to share. For people who get overwhelmed by anxiety, it can feel equally threatening to be asked to take a step back. Both of them are also feeling the powerful pull of deeply ingrained protections. Acknowledging all this can help couples find compassion for each other, and that is a big step toward reconnection. When they do begin to either open or slow down, they likely find that each of them is feeling something very similar: the physical sensations of fear. Speaking about this together can further deepen empathy and connection. Gradually, both are moving out of sympathetic disconnection into ventral connection. From here, the picture widens and each person's Little Me has a much better chance of getting what they need. When we repeat this process many times, our brains develop a whole new way of being in relationship with another, of loving and being loved. It bears repeating that this is a raggedy, messy, and sometimes painful process, with some days going much better than others. When we stop expecting some kind of linear process of improvement and feel content with something that looks more like a spiral, we are really settling into a long-term, mutually healing, deliciously interdependent relationship.

Let me share a personal story to show you what I mean. After my divorce, I did quite a bit of healing work. But the truth is that once an anxious person, always an anxious person to some degree. In addition to our core wounds, we also have tendencies, and for most of us who are anxious, our systems will always respond in a similar way when something scary happens. While this happens with less intensity and more resources over time, the way we respond to relational challenges will vary from day to day.

Texting has always been one of my relationship non-negotiables, and when I met my current partner, I let him know how important it is for me that he always responds as quickly as he can (within reason). Still, sometimes I'll text him and hours will go by before I get a response. Because he's usually so good at responding, my body starts telling me something is wrong, and it's when he goes radio silent that I can feel the tantrum stirring in me. My sympathetic nervous system is responding, and things can go a couple of ways from there.

I might demand to know what's up, in which case he will likely become *less* willing to share what's going on. This can lead to me feeling like exploding on him. Wherever he tries to hide, I can feel my octopus energy trying to force a response from him to ease my anxiety. Sometimes, the pain feels so intense, my Little Me wants to pack a suitcase and leave, not because I want to run away, but because I am feeling such extreme emotions that my whole body wants to act on them. But I don't act on these feelings because even in the midst of the upset a part of me is observing what has become a familiar pattern. With the help of my inner team, I can gradually find my way back down the ladder of escalation. Over years of practice, I have also learned that judging myself for going back to the familiar pattern only makes things worse. The last thing I need is to add a tablespoon of shame to the mix. So I breathe, make amends with my partner for the mountain of additional texts, and give myself some forgiveness for simply being an anxious human.

If I am feeling a little more resourced, I may be able to follow a different path from the outset. When the text goes unanswered, I can maintain my focus on the bigger picture. I remember that this has happened before, and it usually means he is tied up with work when my text arrives and then forgets about it as he moves on to the next thing. I can tell myself (and believe it) that he loves me. I can also remember that he does not respond well to being badgered. This calls up what I know about *his* Little Me and why his tendency is to withdraw under pressure. I may do some breathing, plant my feet in the earth, and feel like I can ride this out without going into meltdown. Going back and forth between these two ways of responding is part of any growth process.

As well as my own work on continuing to provide a safe haven for my Little Me, I have also had to learn ways to make it safe for my partner to share when he's upset. First, this means reminding myself that he is not going to abandon me. When he backs away, he's just experiencing his own wound. I also help my Little Me recognize that my pain is a response to something old in me, not a result of my partner's behavior. What I have discovered is that my commitment to this work actually allows him the space to process his feelings and work toward sharing why he is upset.

As I am learning this, I can often hold space for both of us until we are able to talk it out in a mature, nonreactive way and get back to a place of connection and understanding. The ability to notice, get inner and outer support, and own my feelings without placing blame helps me not get completely lost in old feelings on even the most challenging days. For his part, my partner has also become aware of his tendency to shut me out, and is doing the work around being vulnerable and communicating when he is upset. It helps me to remember that he isn't pulling away to hurt me but in self-protection because of his own wounds. This awareness keeps me from personalizing it quite so much, so I am more available to work things through. Now remember, I'm a relationship expert who studies this stuff for a living, and I *still* have moments of anxiety when it's a challenge to stay in awareness and regroup. But by being willing to stretch beyond our relationship comfort zones, he and I have been able to sustain much longer periods of intimacy and connection, with the ruptures coming fewer and farther between over time. As we also learn how to repair and come back to connection quicker, we are able to trust ever more deeply that we love each other, even when conflict arises.

While I have a partner with a tendency to shut down, he is also capable of tremendous empathy and connection, and has shown his commitment to our relationship by continually being willing to learn and evolve with me. This was not the case with my former husband, and I cannot state often enough that having a partner who is willing to meet us as we are, anxiety and all, is central to us moving toward deeper intimacy and interdependence. Every time you choose to pause and respond in a loving way, together, you are essentially choosing Team Us.

MAKING SPACE TO TALK

Of course, healing doesn't only happen for couples when times are stressful! It can also be helpful to have open conversations with your partner about the ways you both react to pain and fear (anger, blaming, withdrawal, case-building, crying) when the going is good. Sharing that these are cues that you are feeling frightened or hurt can help you both recognize times when each of you may need help getting back into balance. By taking the time to learn about each other's patterns *before* things blow up, you are making a joint commitment to the intention to repair each rupture as it happens, as you work on a solid game plan that will eventually become second nature.

As a starting place, it's helpful for couples to agree that each person can make requests concerning their needs. "Hey, I'm feeling a little disconnected. When can we talk?" Making a safe space for these vulnerable requests builds a foundation for handling potential ruptures differently, too. You might also make a plan that either of you can call a time-out in the midst of a disagreement if you know you need some space to cool down. When things start to get heated, you might decide that either of you can simply say what you are feeling, for example: "I'm getting angry and need a break. I'll come back in a few minutes, after things quiet down inside me." "I'm starting to feel like running out the door, and want to just sit quietly for a few minutes. Can we talk after that?" Some couples find they need to set a specific time to reconnect for things to settle. Anxious people can more easily become flooded with emotion and are more likely to escalate quickly. If this sounds like you, asking for a time-out can be a vital part of helping you meet a more logical or avoidant partner in a way that you can be heard. The story of Sandy and Kristy is an example of how this works.

♥♥

THE OCTOPUS LEARNS TO SOOTHE

Sandy was a full-blown octopus in her relationship, and her protection mode was to become angry, criticizing her partner, Kristy, and sometimes even throwing things. She shared that it felt freaking good in the moment to let her emotions fly, but that often this would lead to her feeling terrible for hurting Kristy and spending a lot of time cleaning up her mess. Sandy was able to see that even if her anger felt valid in the moment, if she wanted to get back into connection with her girlfriend, she would have to find another way to deal with the emotions that overwhelmed her.

When they came in for couples counseling, Sandy and I explored the fear that drove her into these tirades. She had ample reason to be frightened by disconnection since her parents had been too busy fighting with each other to nurture their five children. Sandy's role had been to try to intervene in the arguments. She would fly into the middle of the conflict and attempt to get them to stop. They never did, but she never stopped trying. Following this pattern, Sandy often tried to fix the rupture in the heat of the moment, but when Kristy felt attacked, she would back off. She needed space to process and would go quiet on Sandy after a fight. This pattern left Sandy hanging, stewing in the anxiety of not knowing when (and if) her partner would be ready to reconnect. To help her see why this was so difficult, we went back to her Little Me in the midst of the fighting. Her inability to get her parents' attention created sheer panic. In our sessions, Kristy was also able to see, and even validate, how hard it must be for Sandy when she withdrew emotionally from her partner after a fight.

Together, we worked out a plan for when Sandy got upset. She thought she could say, "I'm hitting anger right now because I'm upset and I need some space to calm down." She would follow this with a request: "Can we set up a time when you will connect with me about this? I love you and I need some reassurance that you're here for me." For her part, Kristy said that would help her feel safe enough to set up a time to talk, perhaps after a few hours, or sometimes even the next day. She felt comfortable letting Sandy know, "You are important to me. I love you. I need some time to process and then we can talk."

The intention in them having this exchange, including setting a specific time to come back together to repair the rupture, was to offer each other the reassurance that they were equally committed to the relationship. For Sandy, this helped her know that her needs were important to Kristy and that they were going to repair this. Her Little Me could hear how different this was from the emotional neglect she experienced in her childhood. This stopped her from spiraling, so she could spend time with the support of her Inner Nurturers and listen to Little Me to continue healing this core wound. Kristy also felt it was safer to open up when she could sense Sandy cooling down. Sandy needed to know she was important and that Kristy was as committed to the relationship as she was, and Kristy needed permission to process and regroup. Creating a clear structure for this process in advance helped both of them feel safe and secure enough to not bring out their familiar protections. They were more able to stay in connection from the time of the rupture until the repair. With a number of months of dedicated practice, Sandy found she felt safe enough that she could directly say to Kristy, "I'm feeling scared like when I was five years old and my parents were screaming. Could you hold me?" This was something Kristy could do with a full heart.

The octopus energy has calmed down while the turtle energy has become more vulnerable, making it possible to come back into a ventral state of connection for repair.

When the octopus learns to contain her nervous system with calm and the turtle learns to stretch her neck out with vulnerability, both partners can come back into a ventral state of open connection so they can repair the misunderstanding. Of course, getting to this place is a lot easier said than done, and can be particularly hard in the heat of the moment and at the beginning of developing new responses. If couples have come up with a game plan and one of them has asked for a time-out, the exercise below, drawn from Imago Relationship Therapy, creates further structure for how to communicate when they come back together. While the emphasis is on developing understanding and empathy for each other's needs, it often leads to a solution to whatever caused the rupture in the first place as a by-product of sharing this openhearted communication.

EXERCISE:
TEAM BUILDING FOR TEAM US

First, set a time to talk with your partner to repair the rupture. To do this, you will need to be calm enough to connect and share from a place of no blame, so before you attempt this, make sure you've had enough time to move out of the sympathetic activation and into a ventral state. Remember, if you are having an extreme response, your wounded Little Me is reexperiencing some moments of pain and fear. To discover why, trace whatever you are feeling back to its root as best you can, so you can sense that the big emotions are coming from this earlier experience and not entirely from your partner's words or actions. Ideally, this will happen on both sides during the time-out. If one person models taking ownership of his or her own feelings, the other one is more likely to do the same.

1. When you've cooled down and you're ready to talk it out face-to-face with your partner, center yourself in your heart. Make sure you stay anchored here by breathing deep into your chest. Remind yourself: "We are on the same team."

2. To begin, think about the things you appreciate about each other and say them out loud. You can each share as many things as you like. I know this sounds like a big ask at a time when you might be upset with each other, but this will help lower your defenses and keep you in an open and empathetic state where you can connect.

3. Take turns sharing about why you're upset, using the timer on your phone. When it's your turn to share, speak for three minutes or less and use "I statements" as much as possible. For example: "I feel afraid you don't love me when you don't text me back." If you are aware of any feelings connected to what you experienced as a child, you can also share this. Don't blame your partner for your feelings. Simply let them know they are stepping on an old wound.

4. Now it is your partner's turn to repeat what they heard, followed by asking if he or she heard you right. No debating, no reframing. In Imago Relationship Therapy, we call this *mirroring* or *reflective listening*.

5. When one of you has spoken and the other one has listened and reflected back what he or she heard, switch places. It is

both of your jobs to really see, hear, and stay attuned to what is going on for your partner as best you can, activating what's called *resonance circuitry* in your brain, enabling you to empathize with the other person's experience.

6. As an additional step, the listener can add some words of validation; for example: "It makes sense you felt that way given what you shared." Remember, all feelings are true and you don't have to agree with someone to validate what they are experiencing.

7. Once you've both had a chance to really hear and validate each other's experience, you may even be able to come up with a solution. This might be something tangible and actionable, or it may just mean letting each other know that you are ready to be more mindful of each other's needs as you move forward.

It's amazing how healing it is to have your partner mirror you, and this simple exercise can help heal the old wounds of not being seen, heard, or validated. Your partner is now becoming one of your Inner Nurturers' voices and will be with you even when the two of you aren't physically together. I've seen this exercise alone transform relationships, as couples become much less likely to blame each other for how they are feeling and more willing to open up, be vulnerable, and build a deeper intimacy with each other.

LOVING THE WHOLE PERSON

We began this chapter by acknowledging that there's no such thing as a "perfect" human being. We all have our wounds, and when two people come together, it is inevitable that we will bump up against each other's tender parts at some point. The key to forming lasting, secure, and intimate connections with others lies in seeing each other as the whole human beings that we are, by deepening our understanding of each other's core wounds as children, learning to take responsibility for pursuing our own healing with support, and recognizing that we are all just doing our best. Ultimately, this is also how we learn to give—and receive—the love and acceptance both we and our partners deserve.

Any time you two find your relationship descending into warring camps, ask: "What are our relationship superpowers? What have we gotten better at over time? What have we never had to work on as a couple?" This can be a wonderful conversation to share. Our ANS adaptively tells us to focus on experiences that feel threatening, even when that threat is coming from the past. As we heal, we gain the ability to choose to also celebrate what we love about our partner. This means spending time focusing on the whole person. While our partner might not be the best in one area, reminding ourselves of their positive qualities will help us start to accept this beloved person for who he or she is rather than trying to transform him or her into a two-dimensional love robot who will never hurt us again.

First and foremost, this means both of you becoming self-full and cultivating trustworthy relationships beyond the couple. With this support, you can develop the capacity to hold your center when the storms of anxiety or the urges to withdraw are swirling. From this place, setting an intention to repair any ruptures that arise, however painful, will make it easier to navigate the inevitable ups and downs of *all* your relationships, including with friends, family, and colleagues. Over time, these periods of discord will actually help to build more trust and intimacy while helping you see that conflict doesn't necessarily lead to breakups (aka abandonment). Yes, feelings are tender, messy, and unpredictable, but they are also just trying to show us what we need. When we take responsibility for our core wounds and the protections we have developed to keep us safe, we create choices about how to respond.

Again, this takes time, practice, and a willingness to see what's really going on for both people. Let's close here with another exercise to help expand your care for the whole person in each of your relationships.

Meditation: Bring Your Partner into Your Heart Space

In chapter 4, we did a Heart Scan Meditation to explore how it feels to access heart intelligence and use it to connect with our inner world. This exercise is similar. To begin, ground yourself in the present moment, continuing with the instructions below. You can also listen to the meditation at **beselffull.com/meditations**. Before you begin, find a safe and quiet place where you can lie down and practice going inward.

1. Begin by lying down and taking big breaths, deep into your belly. Fill up on the inhale and release your breath fully on the exhale. Focus on the breath as it moves through your body. When you feel your body relax and settle, begin to guide the breath into your heart space.

2. Feeling full of heart intelligence about your own state, focus on something you are grateful for. It could be your actual beating heart or simply something that makes you smile. Give thanks for this as you breathe it into your heart center. Spend a couple of minutes really feeling the energy of gratitude before you move to the next step.

3. Now begin to visualize your partner. Observe what happens in your heart when you think of your partner. Visualize him or her in front of you or recall their energetic presence. Allow yourself to experience this person as a whole being. If you notice any tendency to judge individual parts, simply bring your focus back to your heart space.

4. Now notice how you feel in your body as you think of this beloved person. Is there openness and connection? Or do you harden and shut down? Simply observe. You don't have to make any judgments about how you feel.

5. What physical sensations are present? In the inner presence of your partner, does your body feel light, gentle, empty, even blank? There might be a tingling, warmth or coldness, or

even pain. Notice where in your body you feel these sensations.

6. What emotions are present? Love, anger, resentment, kindness, fear, or something else? Maybe it's a combination of different emotions. If your mind starts to speed up, allow yourself to return to feeling the sensations in your body. When you feel settled again, let go of whatever emotions come and focus back into your heart space.

7. How do you relate to each other? There may be open space between you and your partner, or there may be an obstruction of some sort, or a sense of overlapping that makes it challenging to tell one from the other. Observe this. What colors and textures are part of the space between the two of you? As you observe it, any aspect of this space may change or it may not. Just allow it to unfold as it wants.

8. As you stay with this sense of the two of you in relationship, what you are experiencing may remind you of past situations between the two of you or from earlier times. If memories surface, just notice them come and go. Then return to your heart space with a breath or two.

9. Once you are back with the space around your heart, observe the flow of energy between you and your partner. If it flows freely, just be with that sensation. If you feel stuck, notice where in your body you feel this. If you allow the stuckness

to be there instead of resisting it, what happens? There is no need to change anything, but just stay without judgment with what is.

10. If at any point, you feel yourself being pulled out of this moment's experience into wondering what your partner may be doing, simply return to your heart space again with a couple of gentle breaths. Then return to your body's experience of your partner's presence in your heart.

11. Ask your heart center for a message and see what comes up. Then ask your partner for the message you need to help you stay centered and see him or her clearly. You may or may not get a clear response. Just offering the question is enough.

12. As best you can in this moment, see your partner as a whole person, someone who is also carrying his or her own wounding, and allow him or her to just be. Then ask your heart center to show you something you appreciate about your partner, and focus on this, expanding it until it fills your awareness. Stay with this for a few moments, allowing your beloved's positive presence to enter your heart space.

13. Then return to the sense of your partner as a whole person and stay there with a sense of gratitude for this opportunity to be and grow together. Allow this image of your partner to dissolve as you return to a sense of yourself as a whole person, too.

14. Rest and relax, absorbing all you have experienced, until you are ready to transition back into the room. Then gently open your eyes.

Because you can experience your partner as present within you as well as outside you, you can begin to sense both a depth of intimacy between the two of you as well as acceptance and appreciation for this person as an individual. This combination of oneness and difference is the essence of interdependence. It's difficult to put it into words, but it's unmistakably fulfilling once you are experiencing it. Learning how to witness our partners and their needs without getting activated by them is part of falling back in love with them in a new, sustainable way, long after the initial rush of romantic infatuation has faded.

So often, I see people trying to change each other and fix something that isn't even broken. In a mutually loving relationship, it's important to accept that some things are never going to change. Communication can always improve and old wounds can heal, leading to some essential changes in the way two people relate, but sometimes we simply have to accept what we may see as our partner's shortcomings. This, again, begins with you: The more you are able to accept all of yourself, the more you will be able to accept all of your partner. Instead of adversaries, you will begin to see yourselves as you truly are: two perfectly imperfect human beings, helping each other heal through more awareness toward ever-deepening intimacy.

CHAPTER 9

The Mysterious Transformational Power of Love

We are nearing the end of our journey together. My hope for you is that you are beginning to understand that while your attachment patterns are embedded in your body, you also have a tremendous ability to heal your wounds, to become self-full, and to attract relationships of all kinds that truly support you. I also hope that you have developed a deeper awareness of why you react the way you do, and that this is because of many factors that are beyond your control. Seeing our full story from this new perspective is how we all start to gain more compassion for one another and the wounds that we all carry. We have embarked together on a healing journey that will change your narrative about what is possible in a relationship. We all have ways we respond to pain. We all carry core wounds. And we all have our own unique story. By working together with your anxious patterns, you are healing them, practicing sitting and tending to your Little Me, accepting your full self as well as inviting emotionally present people into your world so you can develop a felt sense of safety and trust. This is the path to being grounded in the inner security that we all crave and need.

While having a romantic partner can offer profound healing, other supportive relationships also provide a secure haven to help you create a solid foundation to build from. This is because all of our relationships, no matter how we experience them, provide us with a mirror back into our selves, highlighting where healing has happened and where there is healing still to be done. This is a lifelong path that helps us continually evolve toward feeling our wholeness as human beings. By becoming more self-full, you have started to develop intimacy with yourself that will continue to help you foster the types of partnerships that support healing and thriving for all involved. This kind of interdependency is what we all truly desire, and you are well on your way to experiencing it.

YOUR COSMIC HEALING PARTNER

Finding and learning how to grow with someone in a self-full and conscious way while experiencing the deep intimacy that allows both individuals to be themselves is what we have been referring to as the art of interdependency. I personally refer to this co-healer as your *cosmic partner*. I believe that finding someone who heals with you, inviting you to experience a new way to love, is a spiritual agreement as well as a deeply human one. In these kinds of relation-ships, you both learn in tandem. You won't always be in perfect stride with each other, because missteps are part of the process, part of what it is to be human. As we have seen, these moments of rupture become opportunities for repair, leading to an ever-deepening intimacy.

In my experience, finding our cosmic partner happens most eas-ily when we let go, focus on quality friendships and support, and double down on trusting the universe, safe in the knowledge that this person will show up for us when we are ready. Often, that age-old saying *When you stop looking, there they are*, turns out to be true. This is because we are shifting our focus off finding the one who can complete us and allowing all the relationships in our life to heal and support us. Can you see how this increases the odds of meeting a partner who will be part of this process, too? For most of us who are anxiously attached, the constant searching for the one keeps the tension in our system high. This feeling is such a strong reminder of conditions from our childhood that it keeps the old relationship patterns going. When we are with safe people, our system gradually learns to relax and open to the support that's all around us now.

It is also perfectly normal and healthy to desire a romantic part-nership. Learning to focus on all the aspects of building a secure life with other supportive people will allow you to widen your focus so you can prepare yourself for that person to come into your life. If you're with someone right now and there are conflicts, maybe you have an opportunity to understand these ruptures through a more conscious and compassionate lens, allowing both of you to deepen your understanding of each other, bringing you closer. My spiritual side feels strongly that people do, in fact, get sent to us at the right time and that there is a cosmic design to who comes into our lives, including our friendships and other supportive relationships. If you are less inclined to the spiritual understanding of this, relational neuroscience says that we have an inherent thirst for warm connections, no matter how much wounding we carry. In the presence of the right support, we are also primed to heal and find deeper security within ourselves. Each of these warm connections, both spiritual and human, is helping build safety and trust in all relationships, adding to the voice and feeling of our community of Inner Nurturers.

As you are learning this new way to love, your romantic partnership can be about growing together as both of you continue to heal ever-deeper layers. This is the most profound work for both of your Little Mes. For many couples, healing looks like revisiting feelings and situations that cause pain with awareness and skill, so that whenever ruptures do arise, you can experience them playing out differently. For example, due to my experiences in childhood and my first marriage, I was still afraid when conflict (or even a missed text) arose with my current partner. Through repeated experiences of rupture and repair, I came to learn that conflict was safe, that expressing my needs was allowed, and that disconnection did not result in abandonment. In short, I learned that *this person wasn't going anywhere*. I learned that it was okay to express my emotions and speak my truth, and that we could both be two perfectly imperfect humans together. The work we started in chapter 5 about adopting your full self will allow all of you to join with another. This inner intimacy (in-to-me-see) can join with another person who is also developing the capacity to be vulnerable, allowing for deeper support for both of you as you share these valuable and vulnerable parts of your whole self. When I can share the part of me that shakes with fear when he forgets to text back, and he can equally share the part of himself that feels a need to detach when I lash out, we can make a safe space between us to nurture all of each other's wounded parts.

Shortly after we started dating, the man who is my partner asked me, "How long will it take to trust me?" I looked at him and said, "About five years." And I wasn't joking! In many ways I already trusted him, but I knew that because of my past, I would have to learn to trust the *process* of how healthy relationships can unfold. I wanted to make sure we could work through our issues in a conscious way because I knew they would pop up, as they do in every relationship. As I mentioned, I had done a lot of healing work since my marriage ended, but moving into an intimate relationship with a partner again took that work to a whole new level. It was less about trusting him and more about trusting that the universe would support me in the midst of learning the dance of interdependence. I had never experienced this before, not with my parents and not with my first husband. My narrative needed to move from *Relationships are dangerous and hurt me* to *I have this dancing partner to learn with now*. Each day, I had to find ways to let go of my fear and sink into trusting in our commitment to growing together. Over time, the past no longer dictated my actions, allowing me to be more and more present with him in the moment.

Our mutual commitment has gotten deeper as each year passes, as we build more trust in each other even on our messiest days.

Some days are hard still. I think people see us on Instagram and other platforms and imagine we have the perfect relationship. And in some ways we do; not because we have no issues but because we are continually working on them as a *joint commitment*. By now, you know that all relationships are full of bumps, and these can bring up the oldest, most painful feelings inside of us. Idealizing the perfect relationship as anything other than this is a complete setup. Relationships that thrive are not the ones that are all smooth sailing but the ones that challenge us and require us to grow.

As you have embarked on this journey, you will continue to be dialing into your heart's intelligence. Over time, you will notice you are shifting from feeling like you're lacking or different in some not-good way to feeling inherently connected to all there is because you will begin to see that everyone is growing through life, hitting speed bumps and trying to figure it out, just like you. For many of you reading this, I am sure you are in the midst of healing scars from past or even present lovers. As your journey unfolds, you will feel the lightness that comes from holding and healing this old pain.

Science tells us that ninety-three percent or more of our composition is the same as stardust. I love visualizing our supportive relationships as a constellation in the sky, all connected and supporting each other so that we can keep shining bright. When we allow ourselves to trust the universe and our inherent inner wisdom, we discover that something greater than the thoughts and feelings from our wounding has been there by our side, guiding and supporting us all along.

I also believe that a growing trust in your own heart intelligence and in the support of others and the universe will bring you into greater alignment with the path that is meant for you. This may lead to you experiencing meaningful coincidences in your life that can make you feel like you're getting a "wink" from the universe. Psychologist Carl Jung called this *synchronicity*. You know, those times when you find yourself smiling in delighted disbelief, as if events are conspiring to show you that you're on the right path? Everything seems to be lining up without you having to do anything. Maybe it is as simple as you having a question, a want, or a need, and the solution magically shows up at the perfect time. Or you hear that song on the radio that you know was meant for you. Maybe it comes in a book, when a certain quote feels as though it is speaking directly to something you have just experienced. Over time, as you find your stride and build more trust, try to take notice of all the ways the universe is winking in your favor; it will help to remind you that you are always supported. This means along with noticing all the ways in which you have been hurt, it's time to start noticing all the ways in which the universe is offering opportunities for you to grow.

Some people say that when you continue to make this inner commitment to yourself, listening to your heart wisdom more and allowing life to unfold for you, you become like a magnet for love. Instead of your search for love feeling like crossing a desert with no oasis in sight, life becomes more like a river, providing an endless, self-replenishing source of vitality and nurturing. You may get the sense that you will always have enough love flowing in you and this becomes an invitation for others to come join you. You come to understand that love is its own energy and that it never dries up. It is all around you in many forms and in many types of relationships, and it is also becoming a state inside your own being. If this all sounds a bit far out, I want to share Noelle's story with you, which is all about trust in the universe and community.

THE UNIVERSE HAS A BETTER PLAN

Noelle was a thirty-six-year-old client of mine who found she could let go of where she thought she needed to be in her life at her age and instead allow herself to begin to trust the universe. But we began in a very different place. She first came to me in total distress, having hit a period of depression and beginning to use day-drinking to self-medicate. During our first session, she shared that she'd just ended things with her most recent partner because she knew in her heart that he was not a great fit. Now single again, she felt broken and like she would never meet "her person." She explained that when they first met, they'd had a wonderful, long honeymoon period and done a lot of traveling together. It was only after she moved in with him—a big change in intimacy with all that it brings—that the cracks began to show. He could be there for her some of the time, but he never shared anything about himself. She began to feel like she was living with a stranger who was also pretty controlling about things around the house. Over time, he became more and more focused on work, and she spent a lot of time waiting around for him, often feeling like she was in it by herself. With great sadness, she had the wisdom to end it. They were living in California, and when they broke up, she took the brave step of moving back to Florida to be closer to family.

Even though they had parted and she had created some physical distance, her Little Me and her adult self were still clinging to the *idea* of him and the possibilities of their future together. At thirty-six, Noelle felt like her dream of starting a family was slipping away from her. Little Me was so fully feeling her abandonment wound that it seemed like only he could soothe this ache. With both her adult dreams and Little Me so entangled with him, her anxious attachment system was fully activated when she came to see me. Side by side with doing the painful work of healing her early attachment wounds, Noelle and I explored an important resource—the feelings of connection she had with others before she met him. She shared that, right before him, she had felt very content with her life and she wasn't even in a relationship. She was living in an apartment in California with five roommates. She remembers coming home from work and hanging with people at her place. I could see from the joy in her face and the way her body relaxed that she had felt nourished by these connections. Then she met him and eventually moved out of that living situation to try to move forward in her relationship. Sadly, she lost the connection with her friends and the community environment she loved as her Little Me narrowed her focus to this single source of fulfillment.

It was clear that, first and foremost, healing meant helping her become more self-full and finding new support for her Little Me. In addition, her adult self would need to grieve the loss of her *idea* of the life she wanted. To move on from the relationship, she had to let go of her goal of being married with kiddos running around by a certain age. Releasing the fantasy that her ex was the key to everything she wanted meant she would have to accept a simple but often frightening fact: We cannot control every outcome or expect things to happen on a set timeline. When we are anxious, one of the ways we try to stay calm is through repeated attempts to control someone else's feelings, thoughts, and behaviors so that we can steer the ship in the direction we need in order to quiet our anxiety. But this only keeps it running in our bodies like a fever since we are trying to do the impossible. For this reason, it isn't ever as simple as just letting go. It can only happen by building secure resources inside so that we can gradually take our hands off the wheel, step back, and allow the universe to do its thing.

In our work together, Noelle realized that her depression was not the result of missing her ex. She was actually feeling deep sadness about the loss of a dream she had been holding on to about the future. She began to sense that the roommates who had really got her were part of her Inner Nurturer community, and she could lean into them even though they weren't there physically. Because the experience lived in her body, she was able to feel just how happy she was living with those five women and that she very much missed being with them every day. Over time, she was able to see that true happiness was the result of two things: healing her own inner world and making room for family and friends to connect with her. Released more and more from the core wound of abandonment, Noelle could let go of what her ex had come to represent. She could even see that having babies with this partner would have resulted in her feeling even more alone.

As with all true healing, these times of moving toward a future of meaningful connections of all sorts were accompanied by times when she grieved the loss of her dream of starting a family. As the tears came in waves, she was open to more comfort and the cycle of healing continued along with many changes in her outer world. Because of all the support she was getting, she no longer needed the alcohol to soothe her anxiety and pain.

The more work we did, the more her world expanded. But the biggest change, one we might call magical, actually happened when she let go of the idea that to be fulfilled she needed babies on her timeline. Rather than focusing on the unknown future, she was able to be present for what is here *right now*, truly with what is bringing her joy today. She leaned on those who felt like family, and she got a dog. When she brought her handsome three-year-old show Lab to my office, I could feel the oxytocin—the neurochemical of trust—pouring out of her as she smiled from ear to ear. She told me that she didn't know if she needed a man or even wanted kids, as she was so happy just like this. And wouldn't you know, within about nine months, she had a new romantic partner with a ton of positive qualities that allowed them to foster a beautifully interdependent relationship. With ease, they also integrated their new relationship with her family and community. The anxiety that had driven her to cut herself off from everyone but her boyfriend the last time around was healed enough that she could trust she didn't need to do that now. She reflected in my office one day that there was a better plan for her that she could never have known about, and she was so grateful she was supported enough to let go of the old life she thought she had perfectly mapped out and allow the new, surprisingly unimaginable future to unfold.

♥♥

YOU ARE *SO* MUCH MORE
THAN YOUR RELATIONSHIP STATUS

When we become more self-full, we stop chasing ideas of love—what once felt like love or looked like love—and invite love in right now through *all* our nurturing relationships. This begins with staying grounded in our body and remaining true to our heart's intelligence. When we become more self-full, we don't have to fight for love or prove that we're worthy; we inherently feel that we are and we allow people to come in to confirm it. This strengthens the presence of our Inner Nurturer community so that we feel love from within, too. We drop the need to find "the one" or any idea of where we think we should be by this time in our life. When Little Me's old feelings come to the surface, we now have the resources, inner and outer, to listen and comfort them, so that ongoing healing becomes part of our daily life, as natural as breathing or brushing our teeth.

It isn't only our anxious attachment system that puts pressure on us to settle into some kind of relationship on schedule. Our society also tells us how our life should unfold. We should go to college, have a career, get married, and have children. The list goes on, and if we don't want any of this, something must be wrong with us. As a result, many of us feel that if we don't reach an ideal goal, we have failed, or if we get a divorce, we didn't do it right. If we are still single by a certain age, we must be faulty goods. This ideal timeline gets passed down to us through generations. But there is no cookie-cutter template for love. There is not one way our life is destined to unfold. When we embrace our individual path with compassion and understanding, and come into contact with our own wants and needs as they arise, we can get free of the stereotypes and patterns that society tries to force on us. I do believe that our culture is gradually changing to make room for a greater variety of life paths, but the old ways die hard and I still have many women coming into my office who feel the pressure of family norms and society's ideals.

Having a wedding is a beautiful celebration, but it doesn't change who two individuals are or the nature of their relationship. We are all at different stages of life, moving, growing, and transitioning, and all of this is forever unfolding with or without marriage, and even with or without a romantic partner. As we have seen, being single can also be a wonderful place to form loving relationships of all kinds. Whether you are single, on your second or third divorce, in an unhappy relationship, or working with a partner on interdependency, know that you are right where you need to be to grow and to heal.

MAGIC FLOWS THROUGH YOU

On an even more magical level, I also want you to imagine that the transformational power of love can take many forms. While we are meant to co-regulate with our partners, our family, and our support system, we also have the ability to co-regulate with Mother Nature herself. Every day, we are breathing with the trees. Our inhalation is their exhalation, and our exhalation is their inhalation. When we sense this, we can begin to come into contact with our natural interdependence with all that lives. In the 1980s in Japan, the practice of *shinrin-yoku*, or forest bathing, took hold as an antidote to our increasingly tech-driven lives and the toll this takes on our bodies, emotions, and relationships. Perhaps you've sensed that being with the trees changes something in you, and now research proves that this practice can lower blood pressure, decrease levels of stress chemicals, enhance sleep, decrease anger, support our immune system, promote heart health, increase heart rate variability, and ease depression. Most important for those of us who are anxiously attached, our ANS will find soothing balm among the trees. Said simply, two hours strolling in the woods can make us peaceful and happy, giving us the sense of spending time with some very old friends. Leaving phones and cameras behind to better absorb the sights, fragrances, and sounds in the forest (the practice of "forest bathing") quiets our ANS and begins to give us access to the feeling of oneness with all that is. This isn't hiking or exercise, but simply walking at whatever pace feels natural. Doing this, our system practices aligning with the magic of the present moment, something we can begin to carry back into daily life.

Why am I sharing this with you? To remind you that no matter how disconnected you may feel in any given moment, nature herself is always supporting you. For example, my personal experience of co-regulating with nature is in the ocean. No matter my mood, when I enter the warm, flowing water, my whole body feels held by the constant rhythm of the waves. The ebb and flow enter my body, calming me and bringing me right into the moment of still awareness. I am in awe at how the relaxation I get from this movement quiets my anxious thoughts so that I am able to notice every reflection and every glitter of light sparkling off the water. And you don't have to have access to the ocean to experience this. Water has been my nurturer since I was a little girl, as I would swim for hours in the pool or take baths to decompress. The feelings associated with these past memories are equally part of my inner support system.

Let's pause for a moment so each of us can invite memories of moments in nature that have soothed and nurtured us. Where are you? What do you see? What do you smell? What do you hear? How does this experience touch your skin and your hair? What happens to your breathing, your heart rate? These places are each an inner resource because our bodies do remember. Memories don't take the place of frequent hours spent in nature, but they are always there for us in moments of stress. Remembering the rhythm of the ocean can be a sanctuary for me any time I slow down and return to this sacred experience.

This is because when we connect with nature, we are reminded that we are part of something larger than ourselves, interconnected with all that is. We feel embraced in a way that provides safety, we are invited into embodiment by connecting to our senses, and we find a kind of profound intimacy. Being soothed by Mother Nature can become a powerful part of our healing work if we make room for her. She is always there for us, pulsating and breathing in her perfect rhythm, offering her energy to help our system find its way back to harmony.

Of course, we don't always have easy access to nature. At times when I can't dive into the ocean, I simply take off my shoes and plant my feet in some grass. I let myself feel the earth below me, sensing its ever-present support. In just five minutes, I can feel that I am much more grounded. My whole system relaxes, and some of that goes with me when I return to work. Maybe you love water like me and lingering in a bath can bring you into a calm state. Explore and discover what works for you. When you co-regulate with supportive people, partners, and nature, you are fostering a felt sense of safety in your being to help your anxiety dissipate. You are also experiencing one of the truths of what it is to be a human being: We are cosmically designed to depend on many types of relationships for support and well-being.

THE MANY GIFTS OF ANXIOUS ATTACHMENT

A question I get asked all the time is "Can I change my attachment style?" The answer is yes. By doing the inner work of becoming self-full and with supportive safe relationships in your life, you can shift to having a more secure base within. But will you always have easier access to anxiety than most? The answer is also yes. When anxiety is such a familiar protection, reminding you to be attentive so you don't lose relationships, it can always be activated by certain events and relationships, even with many years of healing under your belt. Everything you are learning now, every effort you are making toward healing your inner world, and every new connection you make with supportive people, nature, and animals, will always be resources when anxiety is awakened from time to time.

All you are doing to become more self-full is already changing your attachment patterns by forming new neural connections in your brain and body. By choosing secure, nurturing people to show up for you, you are receiving the kind of support you needed as a child. Over time, you are gaining confidence that you can receive love and support from the outside. You will move into a romantic relationship with more of a felt sense that true interdependence is possible. Since your wounds are in the process of healing, your responses in a new relationship will be grounded more in the present than in past fears and pains.

If the partner who comes toward you has a more secure attachment than you do, the way he or she relates from day to day and under stress will help continue your healing. This person has likely had lots of experience with ruptures and repairs, and is also far less likely to have old pains activated in this relationship in a way that causes big disruption. He or she can be a secure base where you can find safety and a willing partner in the dance of interdependence. If your new person has avoidant tendencies, the two of you will need to be able to acknowledge how each of you is activated by the other and work on healing together. With a willing partner, this is always possible and potentially a rich path for mutual growth.

The truth is that our attachment system changes throughout our lives because of a process called *neuroplasticity*. Since we have an inherent need for warm connections that never goes away, we will always be responsive to new offers of intimacy. Any time we find safety, mutual vulnerability, and loving support in these relationships, our brains develop new connections that support secure attachment. We are never too old for this to happen. When we imagine combining this kind of support with all the healing work being done with our Little Me, the changes in our brain that support security can't help but develop. But rather than focus on changing your attachment style, something that can make you anxious all by itself, I suggest embracing it with some acceptance just as it is right now, and just like you have welcomed in every other part of yourself during our work together. Because the other truth is that being anxiously attached has many gifts.

Having anxious attachment means that you have developed a lot of sensitivity, a big heart, and the capacity to have tremendous empathy. When I used an octopus to explain your energy, maybe you were thinking, "Ugh, an octopus." But these creatures have developed incredible intelligence because they are so vulnerable due to losing their protective shell. They have the ability to change color, shape, and even texture to camouflage themselves, eject a tentacle that is grabbed by a predator and grow a new one, squeeze through minuscule holes to escape, learn to do tasks very quickly, and even develop relationships with human beings. Perhaps you can see how your vulnerable Little Me parts adapted brilliantly during childhood to keep your parents as close as possible and to protect themselves, and now with healing support, they are equally adapting to the love and care they are receiving. When our Little Mes no longer need to be selfless to get their needs met, they can offer their sensitivity to others and provide care with wisdom and generosity from a self-full place. Their inner and outer boundaries will be clear and kind, so they will be able to provide that care and attention to their own inner world as well as to those around them.

An additional gift is that anxious people tend to be very open to change. We are used to reaching out rather than shying away as avoidant people do, so we are more likely to seek others to help us heal our core wounds. Because we often learned that cooperation was safer than resistance in our families, we are more likely to be open to the support of others, while our expanded energies make us more available to the co-regulation offered by the people around us. All in all, the very capacities we had to develop for safety as children make us ideal partners in healing and perfect candidates for the dance of interdependency as the fear and insecurity drop away.

In our Western cultures, we have been taught that becoming independent and self-reliant is a primary value. That it shows strength and ingenuity. But this isn't how we humans are built. As we keep saying, connection is a biological imperative and our whole system has evolved to expect to be in safe, warm relationships. One advantage we have is that our whole attachment style is about making and keeping relationships, even though the core wounds coming from those early attempts have made it difficult for us to trust others. Now, with healing and more learning about what is healthy in a relationship, you can feel good about having needs, you can know that depending on people is healthy, and you can celebrate your natural capacity for interdependency.

In the introduction to this book, I shared my view of love as the most beneficial and transformative energy there is. Love is the thread that holds all of humanity together, the web that creates the universe itself. Moreover, it is our right as humans to love and be loved, and to feel valued, safe, and supported in our relationships with others. All that I have shared in these pages is about healing so that we can do what is most natural and share our unconditional love in a way that includes ourselves and others. We have needed to pause to focus on our own inner world first, to help with the imbalance we have experienced as we've had to adapt by giving our selves away to others. As these wounds heal, my hope for you is that this will spill over into your current and future relationships, helping you not only to attract and maintain the secure and lasting love you long for, but also to connect to something greater than us all. Call this power by a divine name, look to it as your higher self, or worship it as a part of nature, but your work is to heal on the inside so that you can align with the universal force that is love in all its forms.

As our time together comes to a close, I invite you to view the work we are engaging with throughout this book as a spiritual unfolding. Yes, we have covered issues as mundane as dirty dishes left in the sink. We have also confronted the very real human pain of abandonment. I trust that, along the way, you have discovered a love within yourself that you can return to no matter what challenges life brings. And, yes, this is increasing the likelihood of you receiving a truly nurturing and supportive partner to be with on this journey. Please always remember how capable and worthy of true love you really are.

As you continue to heal, my hope is that you will discover the deep wells of resilience and wisdom within that come from having the courage to experience yourself in new ways, and from committing to taking a more compassionate, kind, and understanding view of yourself and your life. From this place, you are beginning to experience a new sense of safety from within, feeling that all those who have loved and supported you are also part of you forever. Please know that it's okay not to have everything figured out. Notice that you are safe enough to not always be waiting for the other shoe to drop. As that happens, you'll find that it's okay to play with life again as you feel your world expand. I hope that you are also reconnecting to the wisdom of your body and that, as you learn how to feel your emotions in a new way by listening to your heart, you are remembering how to fully embody yourself again, as if you have come back home.

As I send you on your way, I picture you walking away from relationships in which you have become selfless and where your needs are not met. I see you feeling safe enough to speak up, no longer willing to shut down any part of yourself in exchange for crumbs of so-called love. I hope that you can see by now that you are worthy of so much more than that.

The journey to becoming self-full is always long and winding, and healing comes in layers. It's not always easy, and sometimes it will hurt. But the joy that comes from accepting and loving your full self is worth all that you are giving to this process. Along the way, you are discovering that finding love is about being love and allowing other support to show you love. Rather than a goal, this is a process that goes on forever as more of your relationships simply provide the safe space for you to share more of what you already have—and what you already are. You are also gaining more clarity and insight around what helps you feel safe and secure at home within yourself, allowing you to connect more deeply and experience true intimacy in both your inner and outer worlds. My real hope for you? That you continue to remain open to healing. That you welcome the support of others on this path. That this support gives you what you need to continue to let the layers of pain dissolve, opening to a new way of loving and being loved. I want to personally thank you for trusting me to be your guide and companion on this part of your journey back to your self and to a life of fulfilling relationships. I feel truly honored to be sharing this path with you—from my heart to yours.

ACKNOWLEDGMENTS

Creating this book has been a challenging and rewarding journey. I began this project feeling pretty alone, but the support I needed started to arrive. Cayla Clark did an impressive job editing the stream of thoughts coming to me as we created the first version. Then there was a substantial pause as I contemplated approaching, with considerable trepidation, the intimidating world of publishing. During this time, Shannon Kaiser was my cheerleader, encouraging me to remember that the message in this book mattered to me. She nudged me along until I found my wonderful agent, Kathy Schneider. Her belief in me has carried me forward each day.

The right people kept coming.

One might say Ruby Warrington is the book's cool-girl voice. We rewrote the manuscript together; with Ruby's support, we began to have so much fun being creative. Thank you, Ruby, for bringing this book to life. Then Bonnie Badenoch arrived as the book's nurturing energy. Her knowledge around interpersonal neurobiology helped ground the book in science, and also brought compassion and tenderness to the healing process that is the central message. Thank you, Bonnie, for not only helping me bring clarity to the content, but also for giving me the sense of reassurance and ease I needed.

Acknowledgments

Thank you to my publisher, TarcherPerigee, for your enthusiasm and care. I am especially grateful to my editor, Sara Carder. You have a keen eye and your suggestions significantly helped this book flow into its final shape. Melissa Montalvo, my project manager, helped me every step of the way, providing steady support.

The book also is filled with the energy of so many who inspire me by their work. Harville Hendrix and Helen Hunt, Bonnie Badenoch, Dan Siegel, Stephen Porges, John Bowlby and Mary Ainsworth, and Carl Jung. Over the years, I have been inspired by too many colleagues to name, who have shared the wisdom of their many years of practice. The courage of my clients inspires me every day as they invite me to accompany them on the path toward healing. I have learned so much from each of you, and what you've shared with me comes to life on each page.

I want to thank my family and close friends who have supported me—Mom and Dad, Blayre Farkas, Alan Stevens, Christina Arcangelo, Licette Sangiovanni, and Gina Moffa, to name a few. Most important, I want to thank Sven Frigger for being my cosmic partner, one who teaches me daily about co-healing. You've always stood by me in ways I didn't know another human could, and you've shown me love I never imagined possible. If it were not for your love, I would never have felt motivated to write this book. You continue to grow with me and love me even on the harder days. My deepest thanks to you, my love.

Life is a wonderful mystery, and I have learned that creating a manuscript for the world to read is full of uncertainty, fear, and suspense. It takes patience in abundance, but most of all, it takes a team. All of you have been that for me, and I am so grateful.

NOTES

Introduction

xviii **A very short definition of codependency:** Melody Beattie, *Codependent No More: How to Stop Controlling Others and Start Caring for Yourself* (Center City, MN: Hazelden Publishing, 1992), 29–31.

xxii **Relational neuroscience also tells us that:** Daniel J. Siegel, *Mindsight* (New York: Bantam Books, 2011), 55.

Chapter 1: The Role of Relationships

5 **Attachment theory, also known as the science of how we connect in early childhood:** Saul Mcleod, "Bowlby's Attachment Theory," *Simply Psychology*, February 5, 2017. https://www.simplypsychology.org/bowlby.html.

8 **The theory of adult romantic attachment:** Phillip R. Shaver and Cindy Hazan, "A Biased Overview of the Study of Love," *Journal of Social and Personal Relationships* 5, no. 4 (November 1988): 473–501, https://doi.org /10.1177/0265407588054005; Sara H. Konrath et al., "Changes in Adult Attachment Styles in American College Students Over Time: A Meta-Analysis," *Personality and Social Psychology Review* 18, no. 4 (April 2014): 333–334, https://doi.org/10.1177/1088868314530516.

14 **According to Porges:** Stephen W. Porges, *The Pocket Guide to the Polyvagal Theory: The Transformative Power of Feeling Safe* (New York: W. W. Norton & Company, 2017), 5–8.

14 **Porges coined the term *neuroception*:** Stephen W. Porges, *The Polyvagal Theory: Neurophysiological Foundations of Emotions, Attachment, Communication, Self-regulation* (New York: W. W. Norton & Company, 2011), 11–13.

14 **When this radar detects that we are safe:** Porges, *The Pocket Guide to the Polyvagal Theory*, 5–7.

15 Now, there's also a third branch of the ANS: Deb Dana, *Polyvagal Exercises for Safety and Connection: 50 Client-Centered Practices* (New York: W. W. Norton & Company, 2020), 16.

16 The ANS begins to develop along with: Dana, *Polyvagal Exercises for Safety and Connection*, 8–9.

18 Ideally, this co-regulation happens through: Kathy L. Kain and Stephen J. Terrell, *Nurturing Resilience: Helping Clients Move Forward from Developmental Trauma—An Integrative Somatic Approach* (Berkeley, CA: North Atlantic Books, 2018), 20–22.

20 However, it is possible to rewire our ability to regulate: Daniel J. Siegel, *Pocket Guide to Interpersonal Biology: An Integrative Handbook of the Mind* (New York: W. W. Norton & Company, 2012), 8-1–8-8; Siegel, *Mindsight*, 5.

23 Besides the fact that close to fifty percent: "Marriage and Divorce," American Psychological Association, accessed April 2, 2021, https://www.apa .org/topics/divorce-child-custody.

24 In intimate relationships: Siegel, *Mindsight*, 59–62.

Chapter 2: The Secret Language of the Little Me Pact

40 Our attachment experiences with our parents: Kain and Terrell, *Nurturing Resilience*, 34–35.

53 Quantum theory shows us that everything in the universe is: Jeff Greensite, *An Introduction to Quantum Theory* (Philadelphia: IOP Publishing, 2017), 19-1–19-15; Zamzuri Idris, "Quantum Physics Perspective on Electromagnetic and Quantum Fields Inside the Brain," *Malaysian Journal of Medical Sciences* 27, no. 1 (February 2020): 1–5, https://doi.org/10.21315 /mjms2020.27.1.1.

57 To help you picture the way energy works: Bonnie Badenoch, *Being a Brain-wise Therapist* (New York: W. W. Norton & Company, 2008), 60.

Chapter 3: The Anxious-Avoidant Dance and More

62 The terror surging through our system: Amir Levine and Rachel Heller, *Attached: The New Science of Adult Attachment and How It Can Help You Find—and Keep—Love* (New York: TarcherPerigee, 2011), 80–81.

66 We could call these *deactivating strategies*: Levine and Heller, *Attached*, 116–117.

77 **Narcissists actually create destabilizing scenarios:** Elinor Greenberg, "Why Is It So Hard to Leave the Narcissist in Your Life?" *Psychology Today*, January 31, 2018, https://www.psychologytoday.com/us/blog/understand ing-narcissism/201801/why-is-it-so-hard-leave-the-narcissist-in-your -life; Craig Malkin, *Rethinking Narcissism* (New York: HarperCollins Publishers, 2015), 134–135.

78 **While it's a term that gets thrown around a lot:** Elsa Ronningstam, "An Update on Narcissistic Personality Disorder," *Current Opinion in Psychiatry*, 26, no. 1 (January 2013): 102–106, https://doi.org/10.1097/YCO.0b013e 328359979c; Paroma Mitra and Dimy Fluyau, "Narcissistic Personality Disorder" (Treasure Island, FL: StatPearls Publishing, 2020), 1, https:// www.ncbi.nlm.nih.gov/books/NBK556001/.

81 **In the very early stages of a new love:** Brenda Schaeffer, *Is It Love or Is It Addiction?* 3rd ed. (Center City, MN: Hazelden, 2009), 103; Siegel, *Mindsight*, 44.

82 **As a relationship moves into the realm of lasting attachment:** Bonnie Badenoch, *The Heart of Trauma* (New York: W. W. Norton & Company, 2018), 115; Levine and Heller, *Attached*, 251–252; Schaeffer, *Is It Love or Is It Addiction?*, 45.

Chapter 4: Listen to Your Heart

93 **We will be moving into deeper connection to our intuitive selves:** Badenoch, *The Heart of Trauma*, 58; Porges, *The Pocket Guide to the Polyvagal Theory*, 15.

97 **Exercise: Heart Scan Meditation:** Lynn Carroll, "Heart Scan Meditation," Therapy Space, permission date March 9, 2021.

Chapter 5: Healing Little Me from the Inside Out

115 **Even better, over time:** Daniel P. Brown and David S. Elliot, *Attachment Disturbances in Adults: Treatment for Comprehensive Repair* (New York: W. W. Norton & Company, 2016), 292.

130 **Interpersonal neurobiologist Dan Siegel:** Siegel, *Mindsight*, 17–19, 227.

Chapter 6: From Selfless to Self-Full

166 **This meditation is also designed to help you relax:** Kamini Desai, *Yoga Nidra: The Art of Transformational Sleep* (Twin Lakes, WI: Lotus Press, 2017), 45–50.

168 One of the beauties of doing this practice: Haiying Shao and Ming-Sheng Zhou, "Cardiovascular Action of Oxytocin," *Journal of Autacoids and Hormones*, 3, no. 1 (November 2014): 1, https://doi.org/10.4172/2161-0479.100 0e124.

Chapter 7: The Beauty of Boundaries

191 Connection is what we're wired for: Lauren Brent et al. "The Neuroethology of Friendship," *Annals of the New York Academy of Sciences*, 1316, no. 1 (May 2014): 1–17, https://doi.org/10.1111/nyas.12315; Julianne Holt-Lunstad, Theodore Robles, and David A. Sbarra, "Advancing Social Connection as a Public Health Priority in the United States," *American Psychologist*, 72, no. 6 (September 2017): 12–13, https://doi.org/10.1037 /amp0000103; Porges, *The Polyvagal Theory*, 284–289; Siegel, *Mindsight*, 17.

214 Author and psychotherapist: Sue Johnson, *Hold Me Tight: Seven Conversations for a Lifetime of Love* (New York: Little Brown Spark, 2008), 21.

Chapter 8: A New Way to Love and Be Loved

223 Research on well-attached mothers and their babies: Ed Tronick and Marjorie Beeghly, "Infants' Meaning-making and the Development of Mental Health Problems," *American Psychologist*, 66, no. 2 (July 2011): 107–119, https://doi.org/10.1037/a0021631; Chloë Leclère et al. "Why Synchrony Matters During Mother-Child Interactions: A Systematic Review," *PlOS One*, 9, no. 12 (December 2014): 11–17, https://doi:10.1371 /journal.pone.0113571.

225 This means having the capacity to acknowledge the old patterns: Harville Hendrix and Helen LaKelly Hunt, *Getting the Love You Want: A Guide for Couples* (New York: St. Martin's Griffin, 2019), 79–81.

Chapter 9: The Mysterious Transformational Power of Love

256 Science tells us that ninety-three percent of our composition is the same as stardust: American Physical Society, "How Much of the Human Body Is Made Up of Stardust?" *Physics Central*, accessed April 5, 2021, https:// www.physicscentral.com/explore/poster-stardust.cfm; SDSS/APOGEE, "The Elements of Life Mapped Across the Milky Way," Sloan Digital Sky Survey, January 5, 2017, https://www.sdss.org/press-releases/the-elements -of-life-mapped-across-the-milky-way-by-sdssapogee/.

257 This may lead to you experiencing meaningful coincidences: Eugene Pascal, *Jung to Live By* (New York: Warner Books, Inc., 1992), 200–205.

264 In the 1980s in Japan: Qing Li, *The Japanese Art and Science of Shinrin-yoku—Forest Bathing: How Trees Can Help You Find Health and Happiness* (New York: Viking, 2018), 57–77.

ABOUT THE AUTHOR

Jessica Baum, LMHC, is the founder of the Relationship Institute of Palm Beach, providing couples therapy, family counseling, and addiction therapy in South Florida since 2011. As a therapist for more than ten years, Jessica has helped thousands of clients with her unique approach to healing, the Self-full® Method. Through her sister company, Be Self-full (beselffull.com), Jessica offers online coaching and transformational courses worldwide that support individuals and couples to form healthy, long-term relationships. Born and raised in Manhattan, she now lives in West Palm Beach, Florida.